good by. Dont forget me. Many kisses
from us all to you my darling. your

Evelyn Rose.

A young girle who was called Evelyn
had just died. She was lying in her
bed coffin, very pretty. All her things
were on the same place nothing
was changed, and even the flower
which she gathered stood in the
glass, but was beginning to fade.
When she died she was only
sixteen years old. There was a
mam who loved her without
having seen her but new her
very well. And she hed to him
also. He never could tell her that
he loved her, and now she was
dead. But still he thought that
when he and she will live next
life when ever it will be, that

The House of Special Purpose

ALEXIS

TSAR NICHOLAS II
Copy of a portrait by Ryepin. It was found rolled in newspaper after Gibbes's death.

The House of Special Purpose

*An Intimate Portrait of the Last Days
of the Russian Imperial Family
compiled from the papers of
their English Tutor*

Charles Sydney Gibbes

by

J. C. Trewin

Stein and Day

Publishers New York

First published in the
United States of America, 1975
Text © George Gibbes
and J. C. Trewin 1975
Illustrations and documents
© George Gibbes 1975

Maps by K. C. Jordan
Designed by Richard Garnett

Filmset by Typesetting Services Ltd,
Glasgow, Scotland

Printed in the
United States of America

Stein and Day/Publishers/
Scarborough House,
Briarcliff Manor, N.Y. 10510

Library of Congress Cataloging in
Publication Data

Trewin, John Courtenay, 1908–
The house of special purpose.

   1. Nicholas II, Emperor of Russia, 1868–
1918–Family. 2. Russia—History—Nicholas
II, 1894–1917. 3. Russia —History—Revolu-
tion, 1917–1921. I. Title
DK258.T7 1975   947.08 [B]   74–30457
ISBN 0-8128-1796-6

Acknowledgements

Our first gratitude is to George Gibbes, owner of the hitherto unpublished documents and photographs upon which this book is based. He is the adopted son of Charles Sydney Gibbes, tutor to the Tsarevich, who after the events in Russia now described and a career in the Chinese Maritime Customs at Harbin, Manchuria, was received into the Russian Orthodox Church, ultimately taking the name of Father Nicholas and becoming an Archimandrite. For many years he ministered to the Orthodox community in Oxford. On his death in 1963 at the age of 87, he left all his carefully preserved documents, diaries, photographs, and many other mementoes of his life in Russia, to George Gibbes, who has made them available for this book, having sorted, interpreted, and put them in order. The book is as much his as mine.

Much gratitude also to Dr George Katkov; to Ruth Gibbes and Wendy Trewin; and to Richard Garnett of Macmillan, who has watched the book through its entire course.

In filling in the gaps in Gibbes's story and setting out the background, I have found the following books particularly useful: *Thirteen Years at the Russian Court* by Pierre Gilliard (London, 1921); *Nicholas and Alexandra* by Robert K. Massie (London, 1966); *Enquête Judiciaire sur l'Assassinat de la Famille Impériale Russe* by Nicolas Sokolov (Paris, 1924); *The Last Days of the Romanovs* by Robert Wilton, Special Correspondent of *The Times* (1920). Others are noted in the text.

Apart from a few exceptions, all the illustrations in this book are taken from originals in the Gibbes collection. Most of the photographs were taken by Gibbes himself and the negatives survive. Photographs from other sources, which include the Royal Archives at Windsor, are acknowledged in the captions.

J.C.T.

Contents

NICHOLAS

ALEXANDRA

OLGA

TATIANA

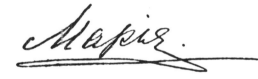

MARIE

ANASTASIA

ALEXIS

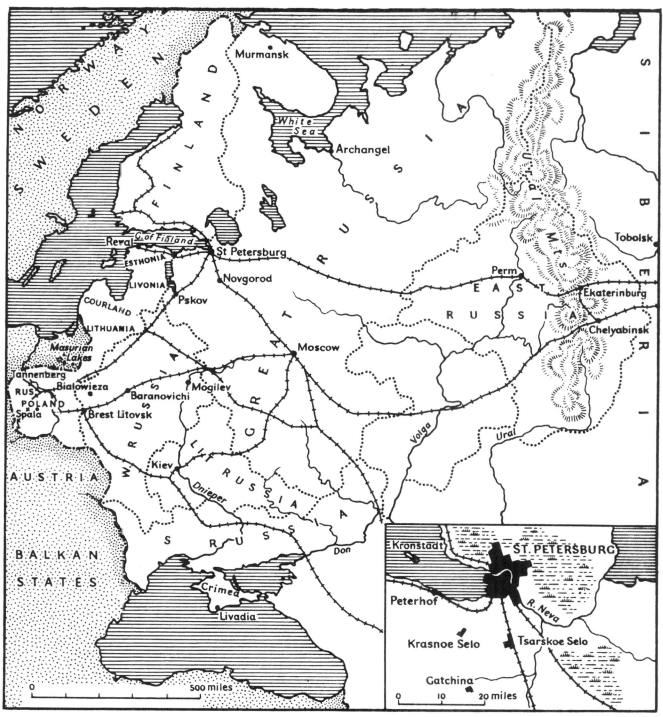

NORWAY

SWEDEN

FINLAND

Murmansk

White Sea

Archangel

SIBERIA

Ural Mts.

Tobolsk

Reval
G. of Finland
St Petersburg
ESTHONIA
LIVONIA
Pskov
Novgorod
COURLAND
LITHUANIA
Masurian Lakes
Tannenberg
RUS.
POLAND
Bialowieza
Spala
Baranovichi
Brest Litovsk
Mogilev
Kiev
Dnieper
Moscow

W   R   U   S   S   I   A

L   I   T   T   L   E   R   U   S   S   I   A

S   R   U   S   S

Perm

EAST

RUSSIA

Ekaterinburg

Chelyabinsk

G   R   E   A   T   R   U   S   S   I   A

Volga

Ural

AUSTRIA

BALKAN
STATES

Crimea

Livadia

Don

0   500 miles

Kronstadt

Peterhof

Krasnoe Selo

Gatchina

ST. PETERSBURG

R. Neva

Tsarskoe Selo

0   10   20 miles

6

Tsar's Weather

All night it had rained; but next morning, the diamond-clear 9 June 1908, crowds in the Estonian port of Reval* on the Gulf of Finland, and upon the heights above their town, were talking of 'Tsar's weather' (*Tsarskaya pogoda*). Reval was glittering with excitement, and the sunshine helped it.

Imperial trains had brought down overnight, from Peterhof, Tsar Nicholas II, Emperor and Autocrat of all the Russias, who was then forty-one; the Empress Alexandra Fedorovna, five years his junior, a gracious, slender figure in blue, who was looking tired in the morning light; and the four young Grand Duchesses and the Tsarevich, Alexis, in sailor costume. With them were the Dowager Empress Marie Alexandrovna and the hierarchy of the Court: gathered to meet King Edward VII, the Empress's 'Uncle Bertie', and Queen Alexandra on the first visit to Russia of a ruling British sovereign. It was also the first time in several years that the Tsar and Empress had appeared before even a small section of their people.

From Reval station they travelled in a narrow-gauge train down a thin spit of land to the quay. The port was elaborately guarded. No one without a permit had been allowed within the dock gates. Even a local merchant had been forbidden, so far, to send out a large consignment of provisions to one of the Imperial yachts.

When the Tsar and his family left the train they saw behind them, on one side, the harbour alive with Russian and English flags, and on the other the parkland trees of the palace of Katherinhall built by Peter the Great. Before them, inside the bay's screening islands, were the Imperial yachts *Standart* and

King Edward VII and Tsar Nicholas II at Reval (Reproduced by gracious permission of Her Majesty Queen Elizabeth II).

---

* Now Tallinn. The dates are according to the western calendar. Russia, at this time, used the Julian Calendar, or so-called Old Style which was thirteen days behind.

The port of Reval during the Royal Visit (Reproduced by gracious permission of Her Majesty the Queen).

Pole Star, and the Royal yacht *Victoria and Albert,* with attendant warships of both nations. Presently, in a clamour of gun-salutes that set every gull screaming above the Baltic, the Tsar, a man of middle height, gentle-eyed and brown-bearded, and wearing the uniform of the Scots Greys, and King Edward, portly in the uniform of the Kiev Dragoons, exchanged their formal visits. At one o'clock all assembled for luncheon among the massed flowers in the *Pole Star.* Only Alexandra Fedorovna, fatigued by her journey, was absent.

Thereafter, for two serene days, governed by unbreakable protocol, the meetings that Russian newspapers were ready to acclaim as a 'feast of peace', alternated between the yachts. At night nothing disturbed the waters of the Gulf of Finland. The various warships were ceremonially illuminated; and the visitors saw Reval itself, its dockside, its towered city wall, its silhouetted roofs and steeples, under the glow of immense beacons that blazed upon the Katherinhall foreshore. The western sky was splendid with sunset.

The second day King Edward and Queen Alexandra lunched

in the larger of the Imperial yachts, the 4500 ton *Standart*,
painted in black with a bright gold stripe that ran her entire
length; at the stern, also in gold, a huge Imperial double eagle
crowned a white-centred red shield. That night the dinner was
in the *Victoria and Albert*. The Tsar had been appointed an
Admiral of the Fleet; King Edward, in return, an Admiral of
the Russian Fleet. Tactfully cordial toasts sealed 'a consecration
of the friendly feelings between two great peoples'.

It meant much to Russia. Only three years earlier the
Russo-Japanese war had ended with the destruction of the Baltic
Fleet in the Strait of Tsushima; national pride had been
gravely shocked. Friendship with Britain was important, and after
the Anglo-Russian *Entente* of 1907 on Asiatic questions, the
Reval meeting was a diplomatic stroke as well as a social
encounter. At its end the parties separated without haste. On the
third morning the *Victoria and Albert,* royally saluted, sailed out
into the Baltic. Later the Imperial yachts followed her, the
Tsar and his family in the *Standart,* the Dowager Empress
and her daughter, Grand Duchess Olga, in the *Pole Star*; British

On the Royal Yacht. The group in the centre consists of Queen Alexandra, the Tsar, the King, Grand Duchess Olga (the Tsar's sister), Princess Victoria. The Empress was unwell (Reproduced by gracious permission of Her Majesty the Queen).

ensigns, which had been flown side by side with the Imperial flag, came down from the ancient Dom Kirche and the Rathaus.

Talking on board the *Standart* on one of those June days, 'Uncle Bertie' had said casually to the Empress that neither of her two elder daughters had a very good English accent. (Not that he could have been proud of his own guttural delivery.) Alexandra Fedorovna may have been piqued. As befitted a granddaughter of Queen Victoria – her mother was Princess Alice, Grand Duchess of Hesse-Darmstadt – she spoke perfect English; indeed her Russian had a strong English tinge. Clearly a tutor must be found in St Petersburg for the children: the twelve-year-old Grand Duchess Olga, shy, blue-eyed, and chestnut-haired, and the taller, auburn Tatiana who was just eleven. Possibly it was too soon to worry about Marie, an enchanting nine-year-old, or the tomboyish Anastasia, who was seven. Certainly it was too early for the Imperial Heir, Alexis, an endearing boy shadowed already by haemophilia, the severe bleeding disease affecting only males and transmitted by females, that was hereditary in the

House of Hesse. Not yet four, Alexis had his own suite in the *Standart,* a bedroom and a playroom with his favourite toys, a blue and red kite, a battledore and shuttlecock, deck billiards, and a bunch of straws for blowing bubbles. A sailor named Derevenko had been appointed his constant companion and guardian.

That autumn, after the elegant *Standart* returned from a leisurely cruise among the Finnish fjords, beaches, and islands, Alexandra Fedorovna made some urgent inquiries. She was told of an Englishman named Sydney Gibbes,* working then in St Petersburg and a prominent member of the lately-founded Guild of English Teachers. Within a few weeks he received an unexpected Imperial command.

Alexis, the young Tsarevich, at Reval (Reproduced by gracious permission of Her Majesty the Queen).

* He had chosen himself to spell it 'Gibbes', after what he believed to be an old family style; but in his years with the Imperial Family the plain spelling, used officially, was 'Gibbs', as on his birth certificate. Here we keep to the form he preferred.

Imperial Classroom

Charles Sydney Gibbes was thirty-two, a tall man with light brown hair above a high forehead. Courteous and observant, he was a ready speaker in a precise voice, a good organiser, and scrupulous about keeping the rules of any society in which he lived. A Yorkshireman, he had been born, his family's ninth child, on 19 January 1876 at Rotherham where his father, John Gibbs, from Towcester in Northamptonshire, managed a local bank. His mother (Mary Ann Elizabeth) was from Surrey, the daughter of a watchmaker named Fisher. Besides the premises at High Street, Rotherham, the family had a house in the country at Normanton-upon-Trent.

There had been eleven children, of whom five survived, three following their father as bank managers, the eldest (John) in the Argentine, the second (Arthur) in India, the third (Percy) in Gloucester. The youngest child, a girl, Winifred Adeline, became a clergyman's wife at Lea Marston, near Birmingham. Charles Sydney, the youngest surviving son, went to schools at Broadstairs in the south and at Hornsea on the East Riding coast, where his headmaster found him 'painstaking and conscientious' and 'a thoroughly reliable and gentlemanly fellow'. Between the autumn of 1894 and the summer of 1895 he was a student at University College, Aberystwyth. His father wished him to enter the Church, so Charles Sydney went on to St John's College, Cambridge, where in 1899 he took his B.A. (Moral Sciences Tripos) with honours, after four tranquil years ('a man of high character, good sense, and agreeable manners', said one of his tutors; and another, 'Personally most pleasant; of his diligence and perseverance I can speak in the highest terms').

Though he proceeded to theological courses at Cambridge and Salisbury, he realized before long that he then had no real vocation. He decided to look about for another profession, and

Charles Sydney Gibbes as a young man, before he went to Russia.

Gibbes at work in his study in England. He was a keen photographer and liked taking delayed time-exposures of himself indoors.

his father, predictably, was hurt and disappointed. A number of things interested him, from dance movements to the theatre. The theatre especially. He went with his inquiring mind to any play within reach, and, having a methodical turn, kept his programmes (as, through life, he would keep everything). They varied at the turn of the century between Forbes-Robertson's *Hamlet* on tour; Basil Hood and Arthur Sullivan's new comic opera, *The Rose of Persia,* at the Lyceum Theatre in Sheffield; and at the Haymarket in London a play that only specialists may remember: Mrs Langtry's presentation, with herself and Charles Hawtrey, of Sydney Grundy's *The Degenerates* (a piece she later revived). Max Beerbohm, not in a good mood that evening, found it extremly trite.

Gibbes's languages were good. Probably this and his innate theatre sense persuaded him to go, romantically, to teach in Russia. This alarmed his former tutor at St John's, who thought it a waste of talent and said simply: 'You'll be just a governess.' He could have been little else during his first year with a landowning family, learning as well as teaching; at length he brought his pupil to England, showed the boy something of English life, and duly took him back. Other work soon arrived, now in St Petersburg where he was recommended as tutor to the children of various aristocratic households. Presently he became a teacher at the

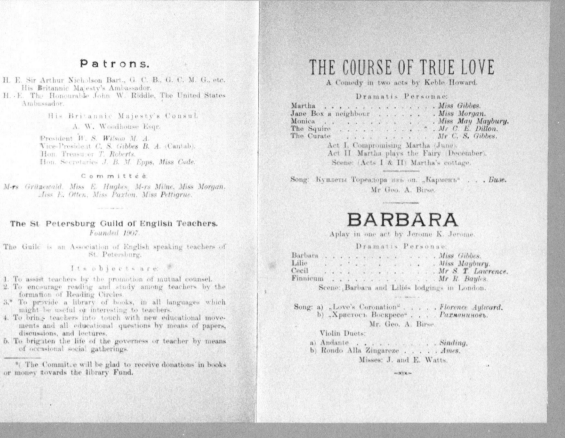

Gibbes had a taste for amateur dramatics. In the second annual entertainment of the St Petersburg Guild of English Teachers he acted a romantic curate.

Imperial School of Law, the Imperatorskoe Uchilische Pravovedeniya, attended only by sons of the hereditary nobility. He disliked the tale-telling that here was rampant, one boy always ready, with a master's tacit encouragement, to inform on another. Invariably, Gibbes punished any boy who came to him with a tale, a reversal of the usual practice and probably startling to his pupils.

Within a few years he qualified as vice-president and committee member of the St Petersburg Guild of English Teachers. In 1907 they got together for 'the promotion of mutual counsel' and 'to brighten the life of the governess or teacher by means of occasional social gatherings'. Two of their patrons were the British

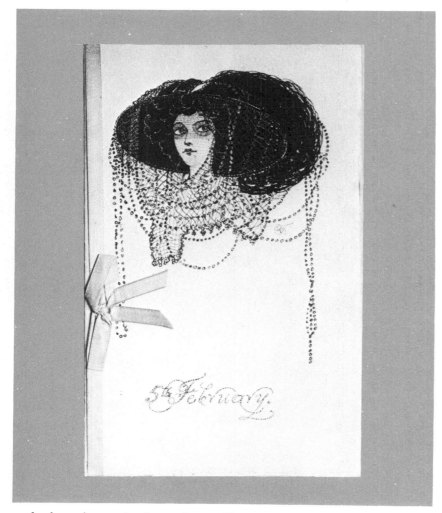

The cover of the programme.

and American Ambassadors, Sir Arthur Nicolson (Harold Nicolson's father; later Lord Carnock), and John W. Riddle. C. S. Gibbes, 'B.A.(Cantab)', was much involved; at a second annual dramatic entertainment and ball at the Comedy Theatre in February 1909 he acted the romantic curate in Keble Howard's *The Course of True Love*, a union of two short pieces, *Compromising Martha* and *Martha Plays the Fairy*. It shared the programme with Jerome K. Jerome's mild and brief *Barbara*.

These domestic matters meant more to the young tutor than the troubled political state of Russia. Since the war with Japan, the Tsar, bred as an absolute autocrat – not a role that suited him, as the more determined Empress knew – had been obliged to agree

A terrace in the private world of Tsarskoe Selo.

to a semi-constitutional monarchy with an elected legislature, the Duma; throughout a vast, amorphous empire, the tradition of centuries was rocking as Russia moved towards an unseen disaster. Its ruler, Tsar Nicholas II, was basically a kind country squire, a man who, for all his charm, had proved fatally malleable. Charles Sydney Gibbes was not concerned with these things until suddenly one morning he was flattered to receive the command to go to Tsarskoe Selo, though he did not meet the Empress herself until he had worked for a year with the Imperial Household.

Tsarskoe Selo was fifteen miles south of St Petersburg. Behind the high, Cossack-guarded iron railings of the Imperial Park there lay a magnificent private world of gardens fragrant with lilac, and vast clipped lawns; a world of lakes, terraces, statuary, grottoes, and triumphal arches. Two palaces were at its core, the immense white-and-blue Catherine, built by Catherine the Great, and rather more than a quarter of a mile distant, the later Alexander, commissioned by Catherine's grandson, Alexander I, and only half the size. The Imperial Family lived in a wing of the Alexander Palace; the Empress had her almost legendary mauve boudoir there, its walls covered with icons and photographs, and above it, approached by a private staircase, were the sitting-rooms, dining-room, bedrooms and bathrooms of the Imperial children.

On a fine day in the autumn of 1908 Gibbes put on the
evening dress then customary for any Court appearance, and
State Councillor Peter Vassilievich Petrov took him out to the
Alexander Palace at Tsarskoe Selo. Here the Grand Duchesses'
austere chaperone, Sophia Tutcheva, presented him to his pupils:
Olga, just thirteen, Tatiana, and Marie, who after all would join
her sisters. Anastasia, at seven, was not yet advanced enough for
serious study; she entered the classroom a year later. Gibbes saw
the Tsarevich only when the little boy came in now and again to
shake hands gravely with visitors.

Olga most resembled her father; the more assured Tatiana,
devoted to her mother, was known to the juniors as 'the
Governess'; Marie was cheerful and lazy; Anastasia, the family
jester. It would be nearly five years before Gibbes had anything
to do with the Tsarevich.

The three elder sisters were simple in their tastes, generally
easy to deal with, and quick if they were prepared to concentrate.
What English they had learned had been from a Scottish teacher,
and it was this accent that Gibbes had to correct. Discipline, when
in the chaperone's presence, had to be at once thorough and
discreet. It was after Anastasia had arrived as a pupil that
Gibbes met his first real problem. Still slightly built (she would
soon grow rapidly), eager in her movements, her eyes sparkling

Anastasia and Marie

with intelligence, she was self-possessed and in entire command of her features; he had met nothing like it any other child. Remembering a course in child psychology he had taken during one of his exploring periods at Cambridge, he tried as many innovations from it as he could; they did not shelter him from storms, usually sudden. Once, after a disturbed lesson, he refused to give her five marks, the maximum (and customary) number. For a moment he wondered what might happen; then, purposefully, Anastasia left the room. Within minutes she returned, carrying one of the elaborate bouquets that seemed always to be in waiting.

'Mr Gibbes,' she said winningly, 'are you going to change the marks?'

He hesitated before he shook his head. Describing it long afterwards in a letter (1928) to the Grand Duke Alexander Mikhailovich, the Tsar's brother-in-law in Paris, Gibbes wrote:

Drawing herself up to the most of her small height, she marched into the schoolroom next door. Leaving the door wide open, she approached the dear old Russian professor, Peter Vassilievich Petrov. 'Peter Vassilievich', she said, 'allow me to present you with these flowers'. By all the rules he should have refused them, but professors are human; he did not. Later, we made it up again, and I received

Tatiana and Olga. They later auto-graphed this photograph for Gibbes.

Gibbes giving a lesson to Anastasia.

my bouquets once more, for the Grand Duchess nearly always gave me one during those early years. I – well, I was more careful in my marking. We had both learned a lesson.

Another morning would not be forgotten. There had been a children's fancy-dress dance at Tsarskoe Selo on the previous night. Gibbes, in tail-coat and white tie, waited at his desk for Anastasia to arrive. When she did, quickly and mischievously, her face was blackened like a chimney-sweep's and she carried a small golden ladder which she placed beside her while she waited for the lesson to begin. Gibbes, deciding to take no notice, was about to speak when he heard a rush of laughter outside the big double doors at the end of the room. They flew open, and through them there appeared the three elder Grand Duchesses with their mother. The Empress looked in horror. 'Anastasia!' she cried, 'go and change at once!' And, meekly, the sweep vanished. When she came back, her face scrubbed as red as a lobster, the gold ladder was still beside her desk; but everybody pretended not to see it and the lesson continued in the Empress's presence. Many years afterwards Gibbes would have cause to recollect that morning.

He had soon begun to know the personal foibles of family and household. The Tsar he saw rarely; when he did meet the Empress, she seemed to him to be beautiful, dignified, and as utterly unpretentious in her manners as in her aspect. In spite of the grandeur of Tsarskoe Selo, the Cossack guards, the ritual, the ranged servants, the Alexander Palace had something of the air of an English country-house, a background oddly right for the Imperial Family. (Though the cooking was poor, no one worried, the Empress least of all.) For the English tutor the months flashed by. Dividing his weeks between Tsarskoe Selo – for each journey there had to be at least two lessons – and his other professional duties in St Petersburg, he maintained his ordered life, keeping exact accounts (every kopeck entered), mixing with the English colony. His hours with the Imperial children were progressively simpler as they grew to know and accept him. It pleased his father – retired now and a widower, for Mary Gibbs had died in 1906 – to hear that Charles had so responsible a position at Court.

In 1913 the Empress asked Gibbes to teach English to the nine-year-old Tsarevich, who so far had refused to speak a word of the language. Some time before this, Pierre Gilliard, an

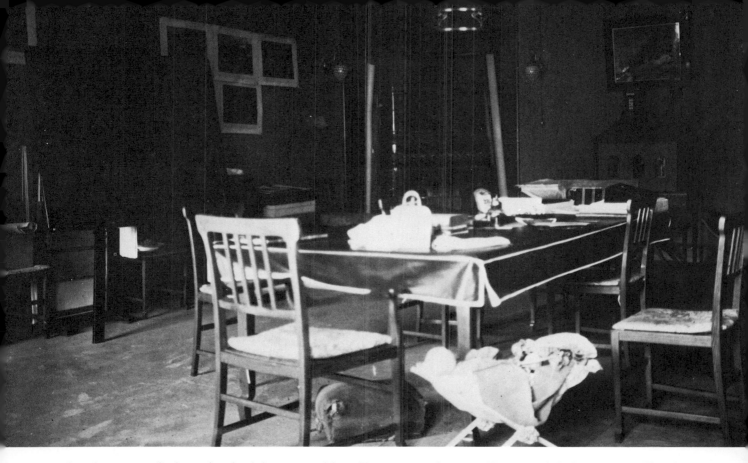

acutely observant Swiss who had been teaching French to the
Grand Duchesses since 1906, had been asked to take on Alexis as
well.

This auburn-haired child (officially Grand Duke Alexis
Nicolaievich, heir-apparent to the throne) would eventually have
to succeed to his father's responsibilities. The Tsar had survived a
series of complex political crises since he succeeded his father at
the age of twenty-six as head of the house of Romanov: in
Maurice Baring's words, as

*The Imperial classroom at Tsarskoe
Selo, with its blackboard and dolls'
house.*

> the last monarch of a star-crossed line;
> Anointed Emperor by right divine,
> From Arctic icefields to the Aral Sea,
> From Warsaw to the walls of Tartary.

There had been the students' riots in 1899, a sequence of
peasants' revolts, the tragedy of the war with Japan, the 1905
rebellion with its general strike and naval mutiny, the birth-
pangs of the Duma. Much else; but the health of the Tsarevich

Rasputin (Reproduced by courtesy of the Mansell Collection).

(a secret that had as far as possible to be kept, and remarkably was kept, from the world outside) continued to be a persistent unassuaged grief. At only six weeks old it was known in the family that the child was a haemophiliac. After any injury, any trifling bruise, the blood would not clot in the ordinary way; internal haemorrhages caused terrifying pain, and often the boy, temporarily crippled, had to be confined to bed. Adventurous by nature, he had to be watched constantly. The Empress, a remote and apparently aloof figure outside her household, withdrew further yet. It was because of the Tsarevich that she gave herself without stint to the Orthodox Church; because of him that she sought for a spiritual guide and responded pathetically to the presumed miracle-working of a Siberian peasant, Gregory Efimovich, nicknamed since youth Rasputin (in Russian, dissolute). Arrogant, filthy and semi-literate, Rasputin – 'man of God', as he was known – was able by some form of hypnotic suggestion to alleviate the Tsarevich's suffering. This crafty sensualist, with his compelling grey or pale blue eyes (one observer called them 'shining, steel-like') became the presumed evil spirit behind the throne and government of Russia. The more he was attacked, the more loyally Tsar and Empress supported a friend whom they held to be the saviour of the Tsarevich and through him, ironically, of the nation. Charles Sydney Gibbes told the historian George Katkov[*] that one day during the war he watched the Tsar opening the Imperial mail at military headquarters in Mogilev. Tossing a letter into the wastepaper basket, Nicholas exclaimed: 'Another of those denunciations of Gregory. I get them almost every day and throw them away unread.'

Inevitably, Rasputin's character has been simplified and melodramatised. He may not have had all the backstairs political influence attributed to him, but he was unremittingly devious and demanding, and his enemies multiplied dangerously. He had no official position; it was enough that he had the Imperial favour. For eleven years[†] he was about the Court. The last five of his prominence – which he had owed first of all to his repeated ability to soothe a sick child – would coincide with the fatal crumbling of Imperial Russia.

[*] *Russia 1917: The February Revolution* (London, 1967).
[†] On 1 November 1904 the Tsar wrote in his diary: 'Today we made the acquaintance of Gregory, the Man of God from the province of Tobolsk.'

Alexis, heir apparent to the throne of all the Russias.

The Sovereign Heir

Charles Sydney Gibbes, asked to succeed where the Empress had failed, had his most urgent challenge yet. In the private apartments of the Alexander Palace he began to teach the child, who was unsure of him to begin with, a little suspicious.

It was long before lessons could get going as Gibbes wished, because the Tsarevich had the most exhausting illness of his brief life at that time. Through 1913, tercentenary year of the Romanovs – Michael, first Tsar of the dynasty, was crowned in 1613 – he was slowly recovering from a frightening attack which had occurred while the family was on holiday in eastern Poland during the autumn of 1912. At Bialowieza he had fallen from a boat and hurt his groin. Pain seemed to diminish, but after a fortnight it returned desperately while the family was at Spala; there had been a grave haemorrhage in the groin and thigh. For many days the boy was in agonised delirium; his parents, distraught, tried (not altogether with success) to keep news of his illness from the outside world. Evasive medical bulletins were published; on a night in October the end was close. Then the stricken Empress had a telegram sent to Rasputin, who was at his home in Siberia, begging him to pray for the Tsarevich. Immediately he telegraphed: 'God has seen your tears and heard your prayers. Do not grieve. The little one will not die. Do not allow the doctors to bother him too much.' After a day the bleeding stopped; why it did has never been logically explained. The Empress would never have believed that Rasputin's message was coincidental: for her he was the instrument of God. Alexis did recover, though he did not walk again for nearly a year, and in Moscow, at the meridian of the tercentenary celebrations, he had to be borne into the Kremlin in the arms of a Cossack of the bodyguard.

From an opening choral *Te Deum* in the cathedral at St

The Sovereign Heir.

24

Alexis out for a drive with his tutor.

Petersburg, the rites had been resplendent. They were indeed the last efflorescence of the Romanovs. They distracted the public mind. They helped, just when it was needed, to renew devotion to the Throne. But they were testing for the Empress who had to move up with the Imperial Family from Tsarskoe Selo to the expanse of the great Winter Palace, a temporary move no one much liked. Weakened after her ordeal at Spala, she could hardly endure a long ceremonial progress (and any fatigue would be noticed and resented).

Once the Tsarevich was about again, although a trifle less ebullient than he had been, his English tutor did not find him overcast by memories of his illness or dread of the future. He was potentially clever and, when free of his shyness, warm-hearted.

Besides teaching him and the Grand Duchesses, Gibbes had a good deal else to do. The Imperial appointment had fortified his prestige; he was now director of some Higher Courses of Modern Languages, with many students and an address on the Nevsky Prospect. It was pleasant then, in spite of glum auguries, to live among the mansions and Palladian colonnades of that perfectly-proportioned city of the North. It had been built on what had been a sour marsh; the Neva ran through it, past the quays and palaces, the gold needle over the fortress of Peter and Paul, the tall Admiralty spire, and the gold dome of the Cathedral of

The opening of Gibbes's journal.

Our Lady of Kazan. Sydney Gibbes was firmly attached to the place, its ice-bound winters of silver and steel, its strange opal nights of high summer. He became equally fond of the park at Tsarskoe Selo and the familiar rooms of the Alexander Palace. Though the Tsarevich's playroom here was crammed with mechanical toys, Alexis had a child's taste for simple things, as shown in a brief journal Gibbes had begun to keep, intermittently, in 1914. He entitled it 'Lessons with Alexis Nicholaevitch', and it opened:

8 January [Old Style]: At desk. By mistake the Priest began first, and I had mine from 12.30 to 12.50. Gave him 'Three blind mice' from *Mother Goose Book,* which he repeated with me. No voluntary effort at conversation. Was most observant of *me* and my clothes and actions. . .

22 January: Looked at the *Golliwog's Circus Book.* He wrote a letter in coloured chalks for A.N. [Anastasia Nicolaievna]. Afterwards we made a paper hat and he showed more interest and said a few words.

25 January: On sofa: foot tied up. Talked about the dog and then showed him new picture-book. Afterwards made a paper hat each, which turned out badly, and then began paper boxes; I showed him one complete. He spoke more English in making the box and asked the questions relative to it in English.

1 February: A.N. [Alexis Nicolaievich] at this lesson suddenly began to walk about and thereupon became less shy and volunteered remarks in English. Generally it was rather better.

3 February: We drew things on the blackboard with eyes shut. Added tails to pigs, and his manner lost much of its shyness.

8 February: During this lesson we played on the floor, and I made him flags out of paper by drawing it and colouring. He coloured one and I the other. Flagstaff was also rolled out of paper and tied with wire.

10, 17, 24 February: During these three lessons we played on the floor. Very little progress. There were too many holidays – Carnival and First Week of Lent.

1 March: We repeated nursery rhymes. Some he said, but with great diffidence.

3 March: He wandered a little, but finally sat at the writing-table. Began the story of 'The Fisherman of York'. He understood very little. A.N. [Anastasia] came in from Music and explained in Russian.

On 3 March, about 6.40 in the evening, when Gibbes was teaching Grand Duchess Marie, the Empress herself appeared and sat until nearly seven o'clock. Gibbes was a little embarrassed:

Watercolours of Russian landscapes by the Grand Duchesses.

Chandelier from the House of Special Purpose in Ekaterinburg where the Imperial Family was murdered. It now hangs in the chapel in St Nicholas House, Oxford.

The chapel in St Nicholas House, with many of Gibbes's treasures.

Having given H.M. a chair, I took one, and then, feeling uncertain about the etiquette, stood up, the dictation-book lying on the table. H.M. remarked on this and thought it was a source of danger. I assured H.M. that [Marie] never looked, or, if she did, always confessed immediately. Still, H.M. said, it is a great temptation (of course, when sitting, I generally hold the book in my hand). I asked whether H.M. had noticed an improvement. She said [Marie] had told her; but—from the little notes I received—she didn't seem to have done so . . .

The conversation turned on the lesson with A.N. [the Tsarevich], and H.M. asked me what progress he was making. I said it was slow and difficult work, and that sometimes he said extremely little. I explained that at first he said nothing at all. The first time he seemed only to watch me and take in details of my dress—this seemed to amuse H.M. She said he was very shy and would get used to me, and I said, yes, it was very unfortunate we had such a short time: lessons twice a week for half an hour that was sometimes twenty minutes. Yes, the Empress said, it was hardly worth-while. I showed her the three books I was then using, *Mother Goose, First Steps to Literature,* and *How to Tell Stories to Children,* and she seemed interested.

The Empress.

By the end of the same week the comment was 'Rather better'. The Tsarevich brought in some wire. Gibbes and he cut off two lengths; he made telegraph and telephone wires, and they 'telegraphed' to each other, holding the wire to the ear and between the teeth:

He seemed very surprised to hear with his teeth. Then I continued the story of the 'Fish and the Ring', and when I repeated it, he seemed to remember it and certainly replied better when I asked him questions . . . In the middle of the hour he asked permission to ring for Derevenko whom he asked for sweets. The sailor returned bringing a chocolate in a glass which the infant ate with relish. The habit has begun and ought to be stopped. It is piggish to eat like that in company.

On Monday, 10 March, they could have only a fifteen-minute lesson in the early evening; Alexis was making whips all the time, with Gibbes's help, but 'he talked English more or less . . . He was perhaps more friendly disposed. He has a nice little face and a very winning smile.' Four days later Grand Duchess Olga, who was now sixteen, finished her last test, a dictation from Oscar Wilde's *Selfish Giant,* and a composition. 'The dictation was quite unaided. I can't say quite as much for the latter. We were

Anastasia at her lessons on the Empress's balcony.

very merry over it, and I am sorry to think our lessons are nearly done, for with few exceptions they were invariably pleasant.' Next day Alexis, far from well, lay on the sofa, listening attentively to the end of the story of the 'Fish and the Ring'. When Gibbes had finished, the boy, who had clearly understood it, said laconically: 'Another.' So Gibbes told him 'The Cap of Rushes'.

17 March: After waiting in vain for P.V. [Petrov] to come out, I opened the door at 5.40, and even then I couldn't get straight off to work, for the lesson had been answering questions in writing, and the little fellow was tired. Then, when P.V. did go, I had rather a bad quarter. First, he cut up bread with his scissors, then it had to be thrown to the birds, the casement opened for him to get up and down, and afterwards shut, rather nervous work. Then he would twist wire round his teeth and wanted to do the same to mine, but naturally I was afraid. Worst of all, he got the scissors again and would insist on cutting or pretending to cut everything. The more I tried to prevent him, the more he shrieked with delight. He doesn't look handsome then: a most curious expression. He wanted to cut my hair, and afterwards his own, and when I tried to prevent him, he went behind the curtain and held it round him. When I opened it he had actually cut some [hair] off, and he was rather disconcerted when I told him he had made a bald place. Then he tried to clip the wall with the scissors and to cut the curtains; and eventually he set to work to take out the lead weights from the curtains. When he had done that, he invited me to go with him to the playroom, but I told him it was almost six. He went off downstairs, shouting out how he had got the lead from the curtains.

Certainly he understands more English, but this lesson was more exciting than pleasant.

Gibbes, who was still totally unaware that the Tsarevich had haemophilia, did not realise how very unpleasant the consequences of any accident with the scissors might have been.

There is now a gulf in Gibbes's journal. When he resumed it in a few short notes, the world beyond Tsarskoe Selo was in tumult. That sultry, bewildering summer he had gone back for his vacation in England, where his father lived in retirement at Normanton. While he was at home, President Raymond Poincaré of France had sailed up the Gulf of Finland for a State visit to Russia: the new French Ambassador, Maurice Paléologue, remembered the jewels on the women's shoulders at a Peterhof banquet: 'a fantastic shower of diamonds, pearls, rubies, sapphires, emeralds, topaz, beryls—a blaze of fire and flame'. Practically at once a deadlier flame rose in Europe. It had smouldered since the murder in June, at Sarajevo, of the Archduke Franz Ferdinand, heir to the Austrian throne. Austria sent a fierce ultimatum to Serbia. Russia, traditionally protective of the Slavs, advised Serbia to make concessions, but nothing would stop Austria from war. The Tsar, in despairing vacillation, yielded to his General Staff and ordered the army to be mobilised. On 1 August* Germany declared war on Russia; in the heat of noon next day the Tsar, who had the Empress with him, replied from the Winter Palace with Russia's official declaration. Crowds greeted it with tremendous and united patriotic fervour. France was at war with Germany; on 4 August Britain followed.

* Western calendar.

Within a fortnight Gibbes received a telegram saying that the Imperial Family would remain indefinitely at Tsarskoe Selo, and would he come? Forthwith he returned to Russia over the Scandinavian route, a hazardous and exacting journey through Norway, Sweden, and Finland. By coincidence, the Grand Duke Michael ('Misha') Alexandrovich, the Tsar's younger brother, travelled on the same train; then thirty-six, he had been heir-presumptive before the birth of Alexis. Few people had treated him seriously, and when the Tsar refused to allow his union with a commoner and a divorcée, he left Russia with her; in the autumn of 1912 he married his mistress, Nathalie Cheremetevskaya, who had already borne him a son. His telegram from Bavaria, announcing this, reached the Tsar at Spala just after the Tsarevich's illness. It seemed that Michael, second in the line of succession, had read bulletins suggesting that the boy might die; hence his resolve to establish a morganatic marriage before he was obliged to go back to Russia. Though promptly forbidding his return, the Tsar had to recognise the marriage and to create Nathalie Countess Brassova. When the war began they were allowed to come back. The Grand Duke was sent to command a Cossack brigade at the front, though the Tsar and Empress steadily ignored Countess Brassova's existence.

Russia's man-power – and, it would prove, her casualty-list – was as vast as her preparations for war were cumbrously inadequate. Even so, at the outset her two-pronged advance through the forests and marshes of East Prussia, one army to the north of the Masurian Lakes, the other to their south, was astonishingly successful. It did not last, and within little more than a month the German generals Hindenburg and Ludendorff had beaten back the premature offensive in two overwhelming victories, the first at Tannenberg. This was the position when, during September, Sydney Gibbes left the city that by the Tsar's order had changed its German name of St Petersburg to the Slav Petrograd and went down to Tsarskoe Selo to restart lessons with the Tsarevich.

Gibbes, on rejoining Alexis, made only a few scattered comments. '9 *September*: Am able to say that I find him greatly improved. Much more developed in every way; brighter and quicker at his work. We spoke most of the time. I told him of my journey, and I also made him describe pictures to me from a comic alphabet.' At that stage the Tsarevich was only too glad

to be distracted. Towards the end of the week Gibbes, as part of some educational method, showed him how to make another paper hat. Whereupon lessons suffered. 'I am afraid the excitement of that was great, and he made several other hats for himself and small friends.'

Alexis playing with young friends in the hay at Tsarskoe Selo.

33

Private Soldier

Alexis in uniform

It was the beginning of a sharp change, a nip in the air. Official duties crowded in upon the Tsar, so many that he could have no time to himself beyond his daily exercise in the park; even this was often cut. Everyone was suddenly far busier.

Discussing the period before the war, H. J. Bruce, Head of Chancery at the British Embassy and husband of the dancer Karsavina, said: 'Except for the Blessing of the Waters at Epiphany, the Emperor, so far as we knew, never came to Petersburg. The Empress I never set eyes on. The only time we met the Emperor at close quarters was on New Year's Day when the diplomatic corps travelled down to Tsarskoe Selo. As a man he appeared to be enchanting. It was his . . . crowning tragedy to be Emperor and autocrat in such times and to be surrounded by sinister and fatal influences which he was probably too kindly-eyed to see, certainly too weak-willed to control.'*

Once Russia was at war Tsar and Empress did come out of seclusion. After the opening months the Tsar was seldom away from his soldiers. The Empress gave herself to the Red Cross. She, Olga, and Tatiana qualified as Sisters of Mercy, wore their habits at all times, and shared in the often anguishing tasks of a military hospital in time of war. The Tsarevich, giving up his sailor's uniform, was dressed now as a private soldier and carried a miniature rifle, made to scale. Only the Grand Duchesses Marie and Anastasia wore ordinary clothes, simple and yet enough (Gibbes thought) to make them unhappily conspicuous. Still, like their elder sisters, they were tirelessly at their chosen hospitals; lessons had to be fitted in when possible. The Tsarevich, to Gibbes's pleasure, was able to study more intensively until a wholly unexpected change.

Though he had left the army to the command of its most

* *Silken Dalliance* (London, 1946).

The Tsar sailing with Tatiana. 'As a man he appeared to be enchanting.'

feared and redoubtable veteran, the gigantic figure of Grand Duke Nicholas Nicolaievich, the Tsar was constantly at the Imperial Headquarters, or Stavka. These were located between the fronts in a forest near the railway junction of Baranovichi. During 1915 Russian troops, who had begun by demolishing the Austrians, met a full German onslaught and were rolled back with enormous loss of life. Throughout the country hatred of all things German had become insatiable; the previous summer's united patriotism had splintered into anger and frustration. The Empress was assailed for her German birth as well as for her reliance upon Rasputin, who was reputed—nothing being too bad for him—to favour a German peace. It was indeed a grim and riven nation when in the autumn of 1915 Nicholas, pursuing what he regarded as the 'sacred duty of a Russian Tsar', resolved to take supreme command himself: an idea that dismayed the Government but pleased both the Empress, who disliked the Grand Duke's authority, and Rasputin, who frankly hated him.

The Empress, Olga and Tatiana as Sisters of Mercy.

ПРИКАЗЪ
АРМІИ и ФЛОТУ

23-го августа 1915 года.

———

Сего числа Я принялъ на СЕБЯ предводи-
тельствованіе всѣми сухопутными и
морскими вооруженными силами, находя-
щимися на театрѣ военныхъ дѣйствій.

Proclamation : The Tsar assumes supreme command.

Soon the Tsar, lonely away from the family he had rarely left, sent for the Tsarevich to visit him at Imperial Headquarters. Later he decided that this should be permanent. Worried though she was, the Empress had to agree, for (she told Gibbes) the Tsar 'refused to go back without the boy'. He believed, too, that to take the 'Naslednik', as Alexis was known, into a severely masculine world would do much for a future ruler of Russia. Moreover – and this was certainly true – the boy's presence would fortify the morale of a responsively loyal army. The Stavka had been shifted by now to the provincial centre of Mogilev, about 500 miles from Petrograd. There, in what had been the Governor's house, Alexis slept nightly in the Tsar's bedroom; daily he was taught by Pierre Gilliard, met all visitors to the Tsar, and played innumerable games with anyone handy. Once the Tsar took him, in his uniform of an army private, on an arduous tour of the entire battle-front. Even if all of Russian Poland and the lower Baltic lands had been lost, the line was stabilised now for the rest of the war.

Sometimes the Empress herself would travel down with the Grand Duchesses and her confidante, Anna Vyrubova, and live for a few days in the Imperial train where she had a large bedroom and mauve-and-grey sitting-room. As a rule, however, she was at home in Tsarskoe Selo, reading the Tsar's regular letters which told her exactly how Alexis was. The news would vary. Any slight injury could be disproportionately painful. In the winter of 1915, after thick catarrh and a sneezing fit, he began to bleed violently from the nose and had to be hurried back, the Tsar with him, to Tsarskoe Selo. Twice he fainted during the train journey, and when he reached the Alexander Palace he was perilously weak. Nothing could stop the bleeding until the doctors managed to cauterise the scar where a small blood vessel had burst. The Empress preferred to thank Rasputin. He had lumbered in, made the sign of the Cross over the bed, looked intently at the unconscious child, exclaimed, 'Don't be alarmed; nothing will happen,' and disappeared. The Tsarevich duly recovered; but he had to stay until early summer at Tsarskoe Selo. When he returned to Mogilev the Tsar tactfully promoted him to corporal.

The Empress reading on the balcony at Tsarskoe Selo.

Stavka

Before the boy went to Headquarters again, Gibbes was teaching the Imperial children for about eighteen hours a week. On alternate days he was Tutor to the Heir, a post he shared with Gilliard. With a fresh interest in games as he grew better, the Tsarevich begged both his tutors to play with him; the man whose service day it was would partner him while the other headed an opposing side. Just then the eleven-year-old was maturing fast. He had persuaded ideas of right and wrong; in a clear, instinctive grasp of possibilities he closely resembled his mother. It could be a curious life for a boy in a palace regulated according to traditional rules that few people knew about. Once when Gibbes and Alexis were wandering through the palace they discovered in an isolated room two men smashing crockery with hammers. It seemed that if a piece of the porcelain kept only for the Imperial Family's use was in any way faulty, no one else could be allowed to have it; and the two men were engaged solely in smashing all pieces that were below standard.

While Alexis was at Mogilev, Gibbes worked with the Grand Duchesses. The Empress had offered him a flat in the Catherine Palace at Tsarskoe Selo. Though he had to abandon some of his Petrograd classes, he prudently kept on his flat there as well; since 1914 he had been concerned with Pritchard's fashionable English School, a property that in 1916 he would buy. But now he, too, was ordered to Headquarters, soon after he had begun hopefully to keep the kind of random journal 'more generally called a commonplace book':

26 July* 1916 : I have been spending my summer in the country if you would call Tsarskoe Selo country; some people do; many, perhaps, do not. It would be truer to call it a ruralised town or an urbanised wilderness, according to the way you look at it. It

Pritchard's English School for Modern Languages which Gibbes bought in 1916. It taught German, French, Italian, Spanish, Swedish and Japanese as well as English, and specialised in commercial correspondence.

*9 August in western calendar.

38

The Chinese cottage, built by Catherine the Great, one of the 'charming palaces' at Tsarskoe Selo.

contains a number of houses and barracks, for it is also a great military centre. But besides this there are many charming palaces set round with vast artificial parks; also expanses of water that have come to seem natural to the place. While that is Tsarskoe Selo itself, the country round it is still in pristine savagery, barren swamp.

4 August: Mr Gilliard has just come back in the Imperial train from Headquarters and telephoned me to go over to the Alexander Palace. There he told me that the Empress wished me to go to Imperial Headquarters to continue English with A.N. [Alexis Nicolaievich]. I felt that something was coming. I was just beginning my supper when he telephoned, and for a while it was quite difficult to eat.

Certainly he was not altogether astonished. In his inquiring way he had been twice to a much-recommended fortune-teller in a Petrograd back street, Konnaya; in effect, the man had said to him (as copied into the few pages of journal):

You are a person who reasons from the heart. You can only be scientific, a pastor, a doctor, a pedagogue, an artist, a musician, a lawyer. On no account go into commerce, it will always prove a failure. You will never win prizes in racing or in lotteries. You are of a type that generally never marries; but, if marriage does take place, let it be an intellectual union, not a union for the sake of face or fortune, for either of these is sure to end unhappily. At present you are

Coming out of the garrison church at the Stavka. Nicholas and Alexis are leading the group of officers.

in an undefined position, but nothing menaces it, it will improve gradually. The first half of 1916 is not good; the second will be better and the first of 1917 also. You will soon take a journey purely on business; it is good, do not refuse the proposal . . . You will never get rich suddenly, but your affairs will gradually improve; money will never fall easily into your hands, and you will receive and pay great sums.

A few weeks later, Gibbes had taken the journey: to the Stavka in Mogilev where the Tsar lived in his hilltop house. Below, the Dnieper ran between sandy banks. There were woods of birch and pine. Gibbes found that the nervous atmosphere worried him a little – life had to be one long wait for the next event – but it was also a friendly place, and the Tsarevich, briskly sociable, said that he was much happier than at Tsarskoe Selo. Though the tutors dined with him alone, luncheon was invariably with the Tsar and the entourage; never less than twenty-four at table, often as many as sixty, possibly more. The schoolroom in the Governor's house could be a reception-room; most of the Grand Dukes (Michael among them) looked in on Alexis, besides Russian and foreign generals, statesmen, ambassadors, 'in bewildering number'. The Tsar would sometimes get Alexis and the tutor to sit with him in his study while he worked. Here once he overheard the boy telling Gibbes that when they went home for good he was going to take the big cut-glass ball that hung from the electric chandelier. 'Alexis!' shouted the usually mild Tsar, 'that's *not ours!'*

When anyone came up to see the Tsar, pupil and tutor had to leave quickly through an inner door. This led into the bedroom which father and son shared, each with his own nickel bedstead. Every night at Tsarskoe Selo, when the Tsarevich was in bed, the Empress had said evening prayers with him. At Mogilev the Tsar, slipping in from his study, continued the custom, though, beset by callers, he had to be less punctual.

Gibbes and Alexis would read, talk, or play with an urbane cat. All his mornings the Tsar spent in the Staff building with General M. V. Alexeiev. Few people had illusions about his role; he never claimed to be a tactician. What mattered at Stavka were his prestige and benign authority. His memory was prodigious; a royal memory none of his children had even begun to match. It frequently happened that an officer, reporting to G.H.Q. and invited to lunch, stood shy and perturbed, wondering what to say. The Tsar would enter and walk down the line of guests. Presently, on reaching the newcomer, he would address him by name – not simply his surname, but Nicolai Nicolaievich, Ivan Stepanovich – ask about his regiment, and throw in a detail or two as if it had all been yesterday instead of months, even years, before.

Gibbes got into the habit of noting daily events from the Tsarevich's point of view. Inevitably repetitive, these entries do show the pattern of domestic life at Headquarters, and afterwards at Tsarskoe Selo, during the five months from 6 October (O.S.) that changed for ever the face of Imperial Russia. Thus:

Thursday, 13 October: In the morning lessons and motor drive as usual. Wrote to the Empress. After lunch motored to the old Stavka and played at 'Robbers' in the forest. [Tsarevich] came home not feeling very well; by the doctor's orders went to bed at 6.30 p.m.

Petrov and Alexis sharing the soldiers' food at the Stavka.

Alexis with young playmates at the Stavka before he fell ill.

Very poorly all evening, stomach quite upset. C.S.G. [Gibbes] read, but with difficulty could pay any attention.

Saturday, 15/28 October : Stayed in bed until lunch. Wrote to the Empress. Lunched in the dining-room with everybody. After lunch played in the garden with Dr Derevenko and C.S.G., then played with soldiers, and P.V.P. [Petrov] read until dinner time. To bed early.

Tuesday, 18/31 October : No lessons as the [Imperial] train [Tsar going on a journey] left at half-past twelve. Doctor came to dress nose and received a present of gold watch and chain. In the train after lunch played at '*Nain jaune*' with the Emperor, Gen. [V.N.] Voeikov [Commandant of the Palace], P.G. [Gilliard] and C.S.G. After dinner constructed the geometrical puzzle, and C.S.G. read.

Thursday, 3/16 November : Remained in bed all day owing to swelling on right leg. Had Russian lesson before dinner. Played with the geometrical puzzle.

The Tsarevich had strained a vein in the upper part of his right leg. On the next day the Tsar wrote to the Empress: 'Baby's leg hurt from time to time, and he cannot get off to sleep the first part of the night. When I come to bed he tries not to groan.' Diary:

Tuesday, 8/21 November : Feeling much better. Slept well and in good spirits, but not allowed to get up until tomorrow . . . After dinner was carried into the Emperor's study, bed and all, while the room was aired. While there was visited by the Grand Duke Nicholas and the Grand Duke Peter.

The Empress had come for a brief visit:

Tuesday, 15/28 November : Lessons in the morning as usual. Motored

Alexis with friends at the Stavka. Petrov is on the left, and Nagorny, his devoted sailor-servant, on the right.

to the train. After lunch motored for about eight versts; the basket carriage and pair of ponies having been sent on in advance. Drove about with the Empress, and played. Dinner at 5.30 p.m., kinematograph at 6. Two new episodes from The Mysterious Hand of New York.*

Thursday, 17/30 November : Afternoon motor ride on the Orshansky road where an exhibition of flying by seven aeroplanes was given. Afterwards played at Robbers in the wood with P.G. and C.S.G. English lesson 5–6, the Empress coming in for a moment . . . Very excited but in good spirits.

Tuesday, 22 November/5 December : . . . Kinema at six. Saw two new episodes from The Mysterious Hand.

They returned to Tsarskoe Selo:

Tuesday 29 November/12 December : Lessons in the morning as usual: Arith., 9–10; Hist., 11–12; English, 12–1. Drive in the Park, 10–11; cold, nobody about. After lunch, rest, and then played in the Park from 3 to 5. 5–6, English reading lesson. Dinner at 6; afterwards, as it was rather cold, played with bricks instead of drive. Downstairs, 8–9; bed at 9.

Saturday, 3/16 December : Russian lesson, 9–10, and then drove in the Catherine Park until a quarter to eleven. Accompanied the Empress to see two operations in the Hospital . . . English lesson, 5–6. After dinner visited Dr Derevenko and played with Colia [the Derevenkos' son, Nicholas] until 8 o'clock.

Back to Mogilev (the journey took 25½ hours).

Tuesday, 6/19 December : Lunched with everybody, 75 persons

* The Pathé Company had presented to Alexis a projector and reels of film.

Alexis with his three tutors, Pierre Gilliard, P. V. Petrov and Sydney Gibbes.

invited. After lunch motored on the Orshansky road and then played in the woods, the pony and sledges having been sent on before . . . Kinema at six. Two new episodes from the Mysterious Hand who is discovered and exposed and henceforth disappears, leaving behind him a mystic ring.

Thursday, 8/21 December: Received French soldier's medal through General. Had photo taken in group with P.V.P., P.G., and C.S.G., and in a second group with the same persons, together with General Voeikov, for General Dubensky's 'Journal of the War' [he was the official historiographer].

Thursday, 15/28 December: Afternoon, motored . . . and played in the woods. Made a shelter by piling snow round the drooping branches of a fir tree. Dinner at 6 p.m. Prince Igor and General Voeikov joining. After dinner played at hide and seek in the White Drawing-room with all the lights out.

Saturday, 17/30 December: Went shopping in the town to buy presents and visited the Hotel France.

Between this entry and the next, the Tsar and Tsarevich had returned to Tsarskoe Selo. The boy was ill again, though Gibbes still did not know the reason, and he never went back to Mogilev. The Tsar had had startling news. Gregory Rasputin, the period's Mysterious Hand, who had been fiercely denounced in the Duma by the monarchist Purishkevich ('an obscure *moujik* shall govern Russia no longer') had been murdered in the palace of Prince Felix Yussupov. It might have seemed that Rasputin had a premonition; he left behind him a strange letter, saying that he felt he would die before 1 January and prophesying doom to follow. One midnight, driving through the snows of Petrograd, he kept an assignation at the house of Yussupov. Five conspirators were waiting, among them Purishkevich and the Tsar's young first cousin, Grand Duke Dmitry Pavlovich. All had been made ready in a splendidly furnished basement room of the Moika Palace; but for well over two hours Rasputin, having eaten cyanide-poisoned cakes and drunk poisoned Madeira, showed no ill effects; instead he insisted on Yussupov singing to the guitar while the other men waited anxiously upstairs. At length, desperate, the Prince shot him in the back; a doctor, who was one of the plotters, pronounced him dead, but Rasputin lurched to his feet, leapt at Yussupov, pursued him up the stairs, and then ran out across the courtyard. Purishkevich hit him with two revolver shots out of four; the prone man was kicked and clubbed, swathed, bound, and finally pushed through a hole in the frozen Neva. When the body was found three days later, an autopsy established that in a last struggle Rasputin had been able to free a hand from the binding ropes. The news of her 'Friend's' death horrified the Empress; autocrat though she was, she had never ceased to defer blindly to him. It was probably less alarming to the Tsar. According to Pierre Gilliard, he had tolerated Rasputin principally because he dared not weaken a faith that kept the Empress alive. The body was buried in a corner of the Imperial Park at Tsarskoe Selo at a spot where a church was being built: there the Empress would go regularly to pray. The Tsar ordered Dmitry to the Russian troops in Persia; Yussupov was banished to his central Russian estates (within a year he had left the country); and nothing was done about the rest.

Gibbes's diary of the Tsarevich:

[Tsarskoe Selo] *Wednesday, 21 December/3 January 1917*: Remained at home and in bed all day, attended by Drs Botkin, Derevenko, and Ostrogorsky. There was no result, the worm remaining in the intestines. Played with the model town all day and with the electric railway. When not in pain, spirits good.

Thursday, 22 December/4 January: . . . Lunch 1, rest after till 3. Went to the Doctor's to fetch Colia and then to the White Tower

Alexis bathing in the Dnieper near Mogilev.

Sir George Buchanan, British Ambassador to Russia (Reproduced by courtesy of the Radio Times Hulton Picture Library).

to play all together. Took Colia back home at 5 and played with him till 5.45 and then home . . .

Sunday, 25 December/7 January: To church at 11 o'clock. Lunch downstairs at 12.30 p.m. Afternoon, went to Christmas tree in the Riding School and helped to distribute the presents. Drove out and played at the White Tower . . . Home to dinner at 6, and afterwards went to P.V.P. to take him his Christmas presents.

Tuesday, 27 December/9 January: . . . At 4.30 went to Dr Derevenko's and back home at 6 o'clock for kinematograph. Saw war pictures, two episodes from The Mysterious Hand, and one comic. During the performance arm became very painful, and directly it was over, went to bed. In great pain all evening.

Thursday, 29 December/11 January: In bed all day, but suffering less pain. The Empress spent most of the day at the bedside.

Tuesday, 3/16 January: Up late, but feeling much better. Dinner at 6 o'clock and played at home at The Mysterious Hand.

Saturday, 7/20 January: Out all day in the Park, playing on the snow hill at the White Tower and with the train of sledges.

Tuesday, 10/23 January: Lessons in the morning as usual. Afternoon played in the park, and home at 4 for a first Nat. Sc. lesson from V.N.D. [Dr Vladimir Nicolaievich Derevenko].

Thursday, 12/25 January: 12.30. Prayers on the occasion of the Saint's Day of the Grand Duchess T.N. [Tatiana]. After lunch out in the Park playing with sledges. Met H.M. the Emperor and all went to the old snow tower and began to clear the foundation of snow.

Thursday, 19 January/1 February: In bed all day but slightly better than day before. Able to play a little and to listen while read to.

Sunday, 22 January/4 February: Feeling better, but in consequence slightly more irritable.

Tuesday, 24 January/6 February: In very good spirits . . . The Empress came both before and after lunch. In the morning sitting in the classroom as the playroom was very cold and only got warm after heating with open fire. Played on the sand table with boats at Naval War. Kinema at 6. The Empress made up models of old-fashioned village.

Thursday, 26 January/8 February: Not nearly so well. Lay down nearly all day and listened to reading aloud, *Robinson Crusoe*. Kinema at 6; after which felt very sick and unable to eat dinner. To bed at usual time, feeling somewhat better.

Tuesday, 31 January/13 February: Very ill all day and hardly able to eat and take any interest in anything. Under the influence of morphia somewhat easier from pain, but somnolent all day.

Saturday, 4/17 February: Visited by the Empress three times. Eating better and in good spirits.

Sunday, 5/18 February: The day passed as usual; in very good spirits. Visited as usual by the Imperial family. During this got rather too excited, and in the evening not quite so well.

Little indeed was well in the state of Russia, certainly not in its capital where incompetence and bureaucratic self-interest had been overwhelmingly destructive and confidence in the central government had expired. Revolution was near, though none hazarded its final form. Military disaffection had grown; civil liberties were restrained; in the harshest of winters a shortage of food and fuel afflicted Petrograd. Soon accumulated fatigue and discontent would shatter into strikes, rioting, mutiny. Early that January the British Ambassador, Sir George Buchanan, had warned the Tsar that he must regain the confidence of his people – a phrase that appeared to puzzle Nicholas – and had told him that the key Minister (of the Interior, and police chief), Alexander Protopopov, had brought the country to the edge of ruin. An oppressive reactionary, he was trusted by the Empress (in a complex nervous jangle after Rasputin's loss) but by few others. The Tsar did not heed Sir George's warning. At this stage, unaffected by his ministers' incredible futility, or simply tired of it, he wanted to return to Imperial Headquarters from the 'poisoned air' of Petrograd. On 22 February/7 March he did so.

Asked in later life why the world in general 'never took the Emperor very seriously', Gibbes suggested that he seemed to be incapable of inspiring fear: 'He knew well how to guard his dignity; one never dreamed of taking liberties, his presence was so quietly, naturally self-possessed. But it evoked awe, not fear. His wonderful eyes (of a most delicate blue) looked you straight in the face with the kindest, tenderest expression. It was his great charm and politically his great weakness, for the inculcation of fear is more than halfway to victory.'

The Tsar, from plaque given to Gibbes by the Imperial Family.

'Nicholas Romanov'

Again, through Gibbes's notes, the Tsarevich at Tsarskoe Selo:

Tuesday, February 7/20: Much better; eating better, especially at lunch when pancakes were served.

Tuesday, 14/27 February: Got up in the morning, but both left arm and left leg were so painful that it was necessary to go to bed again directly after breakfast. Passed all the day in bed. Lunched with O.N. [Grand Duchess Olga].

Wednesday, 15/28 February: Mr Gilliard also in bed, with influenza. A.N. [Anastasia] not feeling well.

Saturday, 18 February/3 March: Played till 12 when the Priest came to administer the Holy Communion . . . After dinner, play, treatment, hair-cutting, and bath. To bed at 9.15. The Empress, as usual, read *Helen's Babies.*

Sunday, 19 February/4 March: Played all day in the playroom; not allowed to go out. Lunched downstairs with Emperor, Empress, and T.N. [Tatiana], the others all unwell.

Tuesday, 21 February/6 March: Still in bed; cough. Reading a new book of Russian fairy tales, a present from the Empress.

Wednesday, 22 February/7 March: Cough very tiresome. Emperor left for Stavka; wrote a short note to put in the train.

Friday, 24 February/9 March: Good spirits but measles more developed. Cut out paper houses and stuck them together.

The 300-year-old Romanov dynasty was about to fall like a paper house. Between 23 February/March 8 and March 4/17 the so-called February Revolution took its anarchic and unpremeditated way. Strikes, processions, revolutionary songs moved into red-flag rioting, shooting by troops (most of them shocked and reluctant), with many deaths among crowds in the Nevsky; then mutiny by the regiments of the Petrograd Garrison which was largely composed of young, inexperienced soldiers, the firing of public buildings, and the storming of prisons. The Imperial Government, such as it was, disintegrated. For a space

Alexander Kerensky (Radio Times Hulton Picture Library).

48

there was neither organised rule at the centre nor organised leadership of the revolt. The eighteenth-century Tauride Palace, home of the Duma, was a sustained babel; one of the rooms held the Provisional Executive Committee of the new Petrograd Soviet (of soldiers and workers) in chaotic session. After nine days a Provisional Government of Russia grew like a belated djinn from the smoke-cloud; Prince G. E. Lvov headed it, and an eloquent and vigorous thirty-five-year-old lawyer, the republican A. F. (Alexander Fedorovich) Kerensky, leader of the labour faction in the Duma, became Minister of Justice (while keeping his place as Deputy Chairman of the new Soviet).

Five hundred miles distant, at Mogilev, the Tsar was slow to react. General Dubensky, his official 'historiographer', recorded myopically: 'A quiet life has begun here. Everything will remain as it was. There will be no move on the part of the Tsar. Only incidental, outside reasons could force any kind of change. There have been "food riots" in Petrograd, workers of the cartridge factory came out on to the Liteyny Prospect and moved towards the Nevsky Prospect, where they were dispersed by the Cossacks.' The Tsar did not appear to be disturbed until a letter came from the Empress late on 27 February/12 March: 'Concessions inevitable. Street fighting continues. Many units gone over to the enemy.' In the next day's dawn his train was bound to the north and Tsarskoe Selo by a longer route than usual. About a hundred miles from Petrograd, learning that revolutionaries were not far up the track, the Tsar decided that the Imperial train should be diverted west to Pskov. It was a tedious, time-wasting journey across the snow-covered country; late on Wednesday (1/14 March) the Tsar reached the empty station of Pskov, and during hours of telegraphic colloquy with Petrograd it was apparent that no more could be done. On the morning of 2/15 March messages from generals on the various war fronts urged the Tsar to abdicate. That afternoon at three o'clock he signed an instrument of abdication in favour of His Imperial Majesty Alexis II, but revoked it immediately after a talk with his physician, Dr Fedorov. The incurable disease from which the boy suffered would put him at the mercy of any accident; further, whatever else the new government decreed, it would assuredly insist that Alexis must be brought up by other hands. Nicholas would not contemplate this. When two monarchist delegates from the Provisional Government reached the train that evening,

Prince George Lvov (Radio Times Hulton Picture Library).

Revolutionary guards stood at the gate of the Alexander Palace. Gibbes was unable to enter

Nicholas told them that he would abdicate in favour of his brother, Grand Duke Michael. A document emerged which included the phrase: 'Not wishing to part with our dear son, we hand over our inheritance to our brother, the Grand Duke Michael Alexandrovich, and give him our blessing to mount the throne of the Russian State.' The delegates set off to Petrograd; the Imperial train clanked from the siding towards Mogilev while Nicholas wrote sadly in his diary: 'All round me I see treason, cowardice, and deceit.' Grand Duke Michael, after confused discussion, himself abdicated within hours, and the Romanov dynasty was over.

At Stavka the ex-Tsar briefly said farewell, begging his assembled officers to lead the army to victory. He had three sorrowful days with his mother, the Dowager Empress Marie, who travelled from Kiev, utterly overcome. On 8/21 March he had a last luncheon – and, so it proved, a last meeting – with her before surrendering to commissioners from the Provisional Government who formally arrested him.

Upon the morning of the following day a car from Tsarskoe Selo station drew up at the locked gate of the Alexander Palace. The sentry telephoned to an officer who came out and cried, from a distance of a hundred yards, 'Who is there?'

'Nicholas Romanov,' shouted the sentry.

'Let him pass!'

At that moment the former Emperor and Autocrat of all the Russias knew himself to be a prisoner. The 'quiet life' had begun.

Palace and Prison

Gibbes's notes on the Tsarevich had continued while Nicholas was absent. Tsarskoe Selo, in this frigid spring, had been plagued by an outbreak of measles, deriving apparently from a young military cadet, one of a group that had called upon the Tsarevich. Alexis himself and his eldest sister Olga were the first sufferers; then Tatiana and the Empress's companion, Anna Vyrubova, each developed a high fever. At the same time the Empress, who had four desperately sick patients on her hands, was further afflicted by news of the rioting and mutiny of the 'February Revolution' in Petrograd. One would hardly divine this from Gibbes's typically reticent entries:

Saturday, 25 February/10 March, 1917: [The Tsarevich] lay very quiet most of the day in darkened room and listened while C.S.G. read aloud Russian fairy tales. Spirits fairly good. Carried in to see other invalids after dinner.

Sunday, 26 February/11 March: Day passed as before . . Spent the afternoon and evening with the other invalids.

Monday, 27 February/12 March: Feeling better, and immediately after waking was carried to other sick room.

Tuesday, 28 February/13 March: Mr G. [Gilliard] telephoned to me on Monday night to say that Her Imperial Majesty said that there was no need to trouble me to come today (Tuesday). A.N. [Alexis Nicolaievich] would spend the whole of the day with his sisters, his temperature being too high to do anything else.

Wednesday, 1/14 March: Went to see A.N. and found him better. In the playroom. H.M. very troubled at not hearing from the Emperor.

Thursday, 2/15 March: Patient better and able to play. Constructed model houses and read aloud. Day passed much as usual. Everybody anxious about the issue of events. No trains to Petrograd since this morning. Slept in my own rooms.

Friday, 3/16 March : In Petrograd.

Saturday, 4/17 March : [Tsarevich] better but not in very good spirits. Knows nothing of passing events, but feels them all the same. We cast lead bullets and built model houses; and with many visits from the Empress and family the day passed.

Sunday, 5/18 March : Patient not quite so well. In the classroom, as there being no water it was not possible to heat the playroom hot-water pipes.

Tuesday, 7/20 March : Patient better, but eyes and ears both troublesome. Spent morning quietly. Lunched with his sisters and slept a large part of the afternoon and had dinner there. After dinner made model houses and played dominoes.

This last note was scribbled down on the night before the ex-Tsar's return. The previous days had irretrievably shattered the insulated peace of Tsarskoe Selo. Outside on the morning of 28 February/13 March a blizzard was whirling snow across the parkland. Northward, Petrograd was in chaos. Though the Chairman of the Temporary Committee of the Duma had advised the Empress to leave with her family as soon as possible, it was unlikely that the rail workers would let them have a train. Not that it mattered, for the Empress had no intention of leaving, and the invalids could not. It looked, later that day, as if the Alexander Palace might be seized. Many of Petrograd's mutinous soldiers had stormed down to Tsarskoe Selo bent on capturing 'the German woman' and her son. Fortunately, Count Benckendorff, Grand Marshal of the Imperial Court, had demanded and received a protective garrison of 1500 men. At nine o'clock firing rattled in the distance, not much more than a quarter of a mile off, near the Catherine Palace, but nothing else happened. In spite of skirmishing during the night the mutineers withdrew on hearing inflated rumours of an immense defending force.

'What is the shooting?' the sick children asked in the private wing of the palace; and they were told quickly, 'Manoeuvres.'

Next day the Empress, waiting impatiently, learned that the Imperial train had been delayed – it was when the Tsar turned west towards Pskov – and a flurry of telegrams brought no reply. (Gibbes: 'H.M. very troubled at not hearing from the Emperor.') On March 2/15, while the Tsar, lonely in the snowbound siding, was preparing to abdicate, Tsarskoe Selo lay in distress: the palace guards had deserted, there were few servants, the house was now without electricity and piped water (though water could be got from an ice-sheeted pond), and both the Grand Duchesses Marie and Anastasia, so far immune, were ominously quiet and pale. (Gibbes: 'Day passed much as usual. Everyone anxious about the course of events.') During the evening of the most testing day of all, March 3/16, the Tsar's uncle, Grand Duke Paul, came with news of the abdication and Michael's renunciation of the throne. In utter grief the Empress collapsed; yet, Pierre Gilliard recorded, she forced herself to see the children as usual so that they might not suspect.

Gibbes on that Friday was in Petrograd; it was clear to him next morning that Alexis felt the pressure of events that no one could explain to him until the Empress wished ('We cast lead bullets and built model houses.'). Alexandra, often in tears, was sorting her private papers. Until that hour, helped by the partly hysterical, partly ecstatic hope that had always worked against her fears, she had not fully credited that Nicholas might lose the throne of the Romanovs. Nor did she understand her deepening unpopularity, fuelled by the name of Rasputin. Gibbes, with his belief in prophecy and divination, was much impressed by a story told eighteen months later by the matter-of-fact Baroness Sophie Buxhoeveden. In December 1916 the Baroness, as lady-in-waiting, had gone on Alexandra's last journey from Tsarskoe Selo as Empress:

She went to Novgorod, a town she had longed to visit on account of its numerous beautiful old churches. Now she had no time to see these, as her visit was mainly to the war hospitals. The Governor escorted her round them, and the nobility gave a large tea-party in her honour, but it was clear to those who were with her that there was no warmth in the welcome, though the Empress did not realise it. She managed to see some of the old church treasures, and the cathedral, and she went also with her daughters . . . to see an old *staritza*, who was over a hundred years old, and much reverenced in the town. The old woman greeted her with the words, 'Here is the martyr Empress Alexandra.' Her Majesty seemed not to hear. She received the *staritza's* blessings and went away cheered and comforted; but those who had been with her came back depressed and apprehensive, for they felt the reception was an omen.*

Gibbes, observing her anxiously, had his reason for Alexandra's failure with her people. On coming to her adopted country she

* *The Life and Tragedy of Alexandra Feodorovna, Empress of Russia* (New York and London, 1918).

Gibbes's diary recording Alexis's illness at the time of the first revolution.

had become more strictly Orthodox than the Orthodox themselves, but one quality she always lacked:

I think [he wrote] it was her want of a 'theatrical' sense. The theatrical instinct is so deep in Russian nature that one feels the Russians act their lives rather than live them. This was entirely foreign to the Empress's thought, shaped mostly under the tutelage of her grandmother, Queen Victoria. When the seven-year-old girl was left motherless, Victoria took her parent's place as far as distance and circumstance would allow; they corresponded until the old Queen died in 1901. Not surprisingly, this fundamental difference between the Empress and her subjects was the basis of the estrangement almost all writers have remarked. She was aware of it without suspecting the real cause, putting it down instead to a 'shyness' which she regretted but could not overcome.

Gibbes had never taken the Rasputin stories too seriously. He regarded the man as a clever, cunning, and good-natured *moujik* who certainly did not go to the Palace as often as angry rumours claimed. The Empress was now concerned with what she later described to Gibbes as one of her life's most painful tasks. All her letters from Queen Victoria (and her own letters which had been returned to her from Windsor when the Queen died) she burned in her sitting-room grate so that no enemy should read them. With them she destroyed her diaries and much more of her correspondence. On 8/21 March, dressed as usual in the uniform of a Sister of Mercy, she received General L. G. Kornilov, who had just been appointed Commandant of Petrograd. Quietly he explained that he had to arrest her for her own protection; that the ex-Tsar would be with her next day; and that once the children had recovered, the Provisional Government could send the family to Murmansk (the only port on the Arctic coast of Russia ice-free at all times of the year); thence a British cruiser could take them to England. Alexandra listened with relief. 'Do what you will,' she said. 'I am at your disposal.'

Next the few members of the household who loyally wanted to stay were put under formal house arrest; the palace was sealed except for its main and kitchen entrances; and a new set of revolutionary soldiers, that of the First Rifle Regiment, was assigned to the guard. Alexandra had yet to take the news to her family. Her daughters she would tell herself: Tatiana, who (like Anastasia) had a trying abscess of the ear, was temporarily deaf and had to have the details written down for her. Pierre Gilliard, agreeing to tell the Tsarevich, began gently by saying that His Imperial Highness no longer wished to be Commander-in-Chief; then, after a moment's pause, that he did not wish to be Tsar.

'What! Why?'

'He is very tired and has had a lot of trouble lately . . .'

'But who's going to be Tsar, then?'

'I don't know. Perhaps nobody now . . .'

That night the snow round the palace glittered under a bright moon. Next day, after the ex-Tsar, as 'Nicholas Romanov', had had an emotional reunion with his wife, he went straight to see the children, all improving now except Grand Duchess Marie who had contracted pneumonia. He soon realised the immediate humiliation of imprisonment when soldiers in the park would not let him walk round freely: 'Stand back when you are commanded, *Gospodin Polkóvnik* [Mr Colonel],' they said. During the evening soldiers in armoured cars demanded peremptorily – on the strength of a resolution by the Petrograd Soviet – that the ex-Tsar should be removed to a cell in the Petropavlovskaya fortress. They were deterred. Finally, in the small hours, other soldiers exhumed the body of Rasputin from a little chapel in the park and burned it.

Pierre Gilliard recorded one of the most strangely dramatic stories. On 21 March/3 April Kerensky (in a blue shirt buttoned to the neck, with no collar) arrived at the palace in one of the former Imperial cars. Gilliard entered in his diary next day: 'Alexis Nicholaievich related to me yesterday's conversation between Kerensky and the Emperor and Empress. The whole family was collected in the apartment of the Grand Duchesses. Kerensky entered and introduced himself, saying: "I am the Procurator-General, Kerensky." Then he shook hands all round. Turning to the Empress, he said: "The Queen of England asks for news of the ex-Empress." Her Majesty blushed violently. It was the first time she had been addressed as ex-Empress. She answered that she was fairly well, but that her heart was troubling her as usual . . .' Nicholas told Gibbes later that year that Kerensky was extremely nervous: so nervous that he seized an ivory paper-knife and began bending it about until Nicholas, afraid that it would snap, took it away from him. Kerensky falsely believed that Nicholas had wanted to make a separate peace with Germany and would hear no denial. 'I knew the Emperor well,' said Gibbes, 'and I quite understand the disdain he must have had for this man.'

The Empress, from a plaque given to Gibbes.

Shut Out

Among members of the household who chose to remain in the palace, and by no means everybody did, were Alexandra's companions Anna Vyrubova and Lili Dehn (wife of the first officer of the *Standart*), both of whom were arrested at Kerensky's orders and sent to Petrograd; Colonel Benckendorff, Marshal of the Palace, and his invalid wife; Benckendorff's stepson, Prince Vasily Dolgoruky, the only member of the Tsar's suite who had gone with him from Tsarskoe Selo station after the journey from Mogilev; Baroness Buxhoeveden and Countess Hendrikov, ladies-in-waiting; Gilliard, French tutor; Mlle Katherine Schneider, Court Reader in Russian; and the doctors, Derevenko and Botkin. Unluckily, Gibbes, on his day off duty, was in Petrograd when Nicholas came back and the palace, closed and guarded, went under prison orders. He had no possible way of getting to the family. Baffled, he called on the British Ambassador; and Sir George Buchanan wrote promptly to the President of the Council of Ministers, asking him to let Gibbes return to work. A reply was delayed. Then Sir George's letter was sent back to the Embassy, carrying a refusal endorsed by five ministers. Gibbes could merely wait impatiently. Nothing glimmered; not a sign from any of the revolutionary officials he could reach himself. Frustrated, he gave up.

During the next five months news of the Imperial Family's plight reached him at second hand. He learned of the soldiers' behaviour, worse when the guard was replaced; of the way in which even the sailor Derevenko,* for a decade the Tsarevich's attendant, spitefully humiliated and left him; of Nicholas uncannily calm, by day shovelling snow, sawing wood, or playing with the children, and at night reading aloud; of Kerensky's visits and inquiry into Alexandra's 'treasonable, pro-German

The sailor Derevenko.

* No connection with Dr Derevenko.

Pierre Gilliard with one of the revolutionary guards at the gate of the palace.

activities';† of the creation of a vegetable garden on the park lawn; and of soldiers' ignorant removal of the Tsarevich's toy rifle. Colonel Kobylinsky, Commandant of the Garrison and also, later, Commandant of the Palace, returned it to him courteously.

A humane and generous man, Kobylinsky watched the family without intruding on them. It was a restricted life. Telephone lines were cut; incoming and outgoing letters were read. Everyone except Alexandra rose early; Nicholas and Prince Dolgoruky walked for an hour and a half in the park (after dusk this was forbidden); lunch was at one; Nicholas, and often the others, would work in the garden until three, when the children had their lessons; tea at four, dinner at seven, and so day after day. Once the Grand Duchesses and the Tsarevich were better, and the depression of their illness had lifted, Nicholas, with Gilliard's aid (*'Cher collègue'* he called him) replanned their programme. History and geography he taught himself; Alexandra, religion; Gilliard, French; Baroness Buxhoeveden, English (in Gibbes's place) and the piano; Mlle Schneider, arithmetic; and Countess Hendrikov, art.

† Colonel Kobylinsky, who had no taste for these inquiries, and took no part in them, said at a later date: 'Nothing was found that could possibly compromise either the Emperor or the Empress. At last they discovered a telegram that he had sent to her. After some hard work in deciphering it, they made out the simple sentence, "Feeling well, kisses." '

'*Nicholas Romanov*'.

Towards Siberia

Because Gibbes had no access to the family – though he still kept his rooms elsewhere at Tsarskoe Selo – he got through what other work he could in Petrograd and now and then harried this official or that in the faint hope of a change of heart. News of his father's death at Normanton in the spring of 1917 was late in reaching him. On 21 April/4 May he wrote to his Aunt Hattie from 4, The Semicircle, Grand Palace, Tsarskoe Selo. Among his papers is a corrected draft:

Aunt Kate sent me the first sad news of poor Father's death; but the letter, written the day after he died, was a very long time in coming, having been almost two months on the way. I have therefore only just had the news. I am sure that our first thought is to thank you for all the love and care that you have bestowed on him during the last years of his life . . . Happy he certainly was the last time I saw him in 1914; so that not having seen the last painful years of his life, I have the brightest recollection of the close of his days.

[Later] I haven't been able to finish this letter before. I have been almost all the time in town with Committees and executing commissions for my colleague; he cannot go himself. I heard from Aunt Kate again (the letter was written three weeks later than her first, apparently; all the letters between are lost) and this time the letter came fairly quickly in about four weeks . . . Nettie tells me that you are going to sell most of the things at Normanton, and I would like to ask whether you could let me have a few things for remembrance sake, especially as it is possible that we come over to spend our exile there. Of course, you will have the things valued and let me know how much it is . . . I am putting a few articles of furniture and a few pictures, just some of the things that are always associated in my mind with home. I am sorry that Father did not live to receive my last letter to him, but I suppose that he knows all the same . . .

I should have much liked to come home once more before all is broken up, but putting aside the question of authorisation to travel which is not given at the present moment, you will doubtless by now know the position in which we are placed here from the turn of political events. It therefore seems out of the question at the present time, for nobody knows what is going to happen, and my duty as well as my interests call for my presence here. Our fortunes are completely broken, and it is more than possible that I shall leave Russia and return to England with my pupil. When that may be I cannot say, for they are not permitted go away at the present time [altered to 'for at the present time they cannot leave'].

Here the important phrase is 'it is more than possible that I shall ... return to England with my pupil'. For months, during Russia's liberal interlude, the Provisional Government had considered plans for getting the Imperial Family to England. Bolshevik extremists had demanded the ex-Tsar's death, to which Kerensky, one of whose first acts as Minister of Justice had been the abolition of capital punishment, answered firmly: 'The Russian Revolution does not take vengeance.' The workers' Soviet did want vengeance; but neither side could move. The extremists were not strong enough to storm the Alexander Palace; the Government could not control the railways. England, in spite of the Prime Minister David Lloyd George's personal discontent,* agreed to give asylum to the Imperial Family if, cautiously, Russia would bear the expense. Almost concurrently, in Petrograd, an equally cautious Provisional Government told the pressing Soviet that Nicholas and Alexandra would remain in Russia. For nearly three months (during which Gibbes wrote to Normanton) the matter appeared to lapse. At midsummer it rose again; now, it seemed, the British Government—for causes never sharply defined—withdrew its offer. Still, whether or not England was the hope, it was obvious that the family must leave Tsarskoe Selo. The Provisional Government was insecure, and if it fell Nicholas and Alexandra must be in great jeopardy.

When the Provisional Government was named after the February revolution, Petrograd Bolsheviks received an uncompromising telegram from Zurich: 'Our tactics absolute distrust, no support of the new Government, Kerensky especially suspect, no rapprochement with other parties.' It was signed Lenin. This professional revolutionary, who would be the true fabricator of a new Russia, was forty-seven. Born Vladimir Ilyich Ulyanov, his

Lenin (Radio Times Hulton Picture Library).

---

* Shared by many English liberals. On hearing the news of the February revolution, C. P. Scott and the *Manchester Guardian* staff had telegraphed 'salutations' to the President of the Duma.

childhood home had been Simbirsk on the Middle Volga: oddly, it was Kerensky's town as well. Most of his life he had been an unswerving Marxist; since leaving Russia at the turn of the century, he and his wife Krupskaya – like him she had been in Siberian exile – had led a voluble underground life in various European towns, London among them. Though in 1917 he had been afraid that 'we older men may not live to see the decisive battles in the approaching revolution', revolution was indeed ignited, and soon. First, he and his party had to dispose of the too liberal and bourgeois government of Kerensky. The problem was how to reach Russia. There the Germans helped. Happy at the idea of raising a dangerous internal blister in a Russia already ailing, they arranged for Lenin to cross Germany in a closed train and to enter Russia through Sweden and Finland. In Winston Churchill's words, 'they transported Lenin in a sealed truck like a plague bacillus'.* It looked as if he had arrived too early. His cry to an all-Russian congress of Soviets for the overthrow of the government and the end of the war was treated with angry derision. Single-mindedly, he toiled on, small and bald-headed, a burning fanatic. Bolshevik authority grew; cracks showed in the government, and at midsummer Kerensky became both Prime Minister and Minister of War. Almost at once, after success on the Galician front, there came a frightening reverse when troops inoculated with Bolshevist doctrines refused to fight. Even so Kerensky contrived by propaganda to quell a 'Down with the War' rising, and Lenin, after the so-named 'July days', had to escape to Finland, disguised as the fireman of a locomotive.

The prescient Kerensky knew that success could not last. Going down to Tsarskoe Selo, he told Nicholas it was time for the family to leave: not to Livadia in the Crimea which had been a vague dream, but to Tobolsk, a town of twenty thousand people in western Siberia, 'an out-and-out backwater' near the confluence of the Tobol and the great Irtysh, 200 miles north of the Trans-Siberian railway. Early in August they would be leaving. Most of the others in the much-reduced household would go except Count Benckendorff whose wife had acute bronchitis; he would be replaced by Count (General) Tatishchev. In the bleak darkness of 1/14 August, two days after the Tsarevich's thirteenth birthday (his father was fifty, his mother forty-five), the travellers were

* *The World Crisis: The Aftermath* (London, 1929).

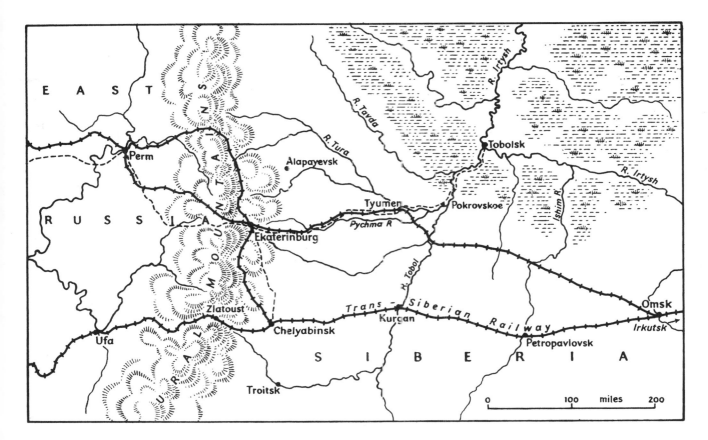

packed and waiting. None guessed how long exile at Tobolsk might last; Kerensky believed that it should end when the Constituent Assembly met that winter.

The wait at Tsarskoe Selo was tense. On the evening before departure Grand Duke Michael was allowed to come for a brief, inconsequent talk with Nicholas while Kerensky fingered through scrapbooks in the same room: an embarrassment for everyone. Owing to rail workers' intransigence the trains ordered from Petrograd were delayed in the small hours. Progressively worried and irritable, the household sat about on trunks and suitcases in the semi-circular hall. Daybreak and no news; at length, between five and six, the sign. Seen off by a few soldiers and retainers, the travellers were driven quickly through a yet unawakened park and the village streets to a pair of trains placarded, ironically, 'Japanese Red Cross Mission' and decorated with Japanese flags. Lukomsky, one of the officials instructed to remove valuables from the palace, had watched the party leave:

The Empress's chaise-longue. She took the bedspread into exile and it later served as an altar-cloth.

Nicholas a sombre figure that morning; Alexis, tall, pale, and joking; the sisters pale also and thin, their hair cut closely after their illness and looking remarkably alike. Alexandra seemed to be crying. Within the palace Lukomsky had to seal as many as forty doors. Finding Alexandra's maid upstairs, packing things away in drawers and boxes, he warned her that this was now national property and would become a museum, even the calendar to be untouched and the flowers left in their vases. All the rooms were photographed, all drawers and cupboards sealed. Alexandra had taken with her much more than Nicholas who left behind practically everything of his own. Many of the family's favourite possessions were on the train; Alexandra and the Grand Duchesses carried with them jewels worth about a million roubles (£100,000). Such minor things as a carpet, lamps, a gramophone, photographs, even three or four water-colours and pastels, would be sent on afterwards to Tobolsk. The trains were comfortable. In the main one travelled the Imperial Family, thirty people or so from the household, a company of the First Regiment, and some of the baggage; in the second, the rest of the servants and most of the soldiers (in all more than three hundred) who, under Colonel Kobylinsky's command, would mount guard at Tobolsk.

While the family was still beginning its eastward course to

Siberia, Charles Sydney Gibbes — or, as he was called Russian-fashion, 'Sydney Ivanovich Gibbes' — with a pass dated 2/15 August from Baron Shteingel, the Commissar acting for the Provisional Government, was able to enter the Alexander Palace and collect the few belongings he had left. Determined to follow as soon as he was allowed, he heard from a now cordial official that there was no reason why he should not get to Tobolsk. He finished his business in Petrograd, disposed of his interests, and was about to leave when a railway strike halted all traffic. No one hurried; no one troubled; weeks straggled on. It was a month before he could feel the train moving beneath him. Behind him were uncertainty and political chicanery; the palaces, the Neva, the wide, rapid river, Tresini's needle-spire on the cathedral at Peter and Paul. Before him, the slow, exhausting progress by rail and water, out into the Siberian heart, to another and a forgotten Russia.

The Grand Palace at Tsarskoe Selo seen across the lake.

Gibbes's pass to enter the Alexander Palace on 2/15 August after the Imperial Family had left for Tobolsk.

65

The Governor's House

Hardly anyone that August beside the interminable ribbon of the Siberian railroad had known about those two impressive royal trains. They were unscheduled on any time-table. Loiterers at shabby provincial stations may have wondered why blinds were drawn and the high cars encircled by a heavy guard. Some peasant in the country silence may have asked, between six and seven o'clock, who were the handsome, bearded man, the tall boy, and the group of girls that alighted, so many versts from a platform, to take their dogs for a run. There had been one brief alarm when rail workers at Zvanko, the first important station on the route, did not want to pass the train through. Over by the Urals the elderly workers' chairman at Perm did ask Kobylinsky what was happening; but he and his friends acquiesced at once when shown Kerensky's signature. After crossing the Urals towards the end of 3/16 August, and a final day on the empty summer grasslands of the steppe, the travellers disembarked at midnight at Tyumen and were transferred to the steamers *Rus* and *Kormilets* for the voyage on the Tura and Tobol rivers. It took them about forty hours to cover the last two hundred miles: a dull enough landscape beyond each bank, though they did pass the village of Pokrovskoe where Rasputin had lived and his house was plainly identifiable. The sun was declining on 6/19 August when the two steamers slid beside the wharf at Tobolsk and their passengers saw the crenellated outline of a hilltop building that dominated the sprawling little town.

Their journey was not entirely over. They had to live on board for a week, so that Kobylinsky, helped by some of them, could look to the furnishing, decoration, and general improvement of the Governor's★ house, the largest in the place. Sturdily unostentatious, two-storeyed, white, and balconied, it stood

★ The Governor of Tobolsk province.

prominent in a dusty street (re-named Liberty Street—Ulitza Svobody) with creaking wooden pavements and many small wooden buildings. The house, which had thirteen or fourteen rooms, could not take everyone. The Imperial Family occupied the whole of its upper floor. The Grand Duchesses had to share a room at the corner, next to their parents' bedroom; beyond this was the drawing-room, and Alexis lived opposite. Pierre Gilliard settled into the Governor's study on the ground floor; but most of the Imperial suite had to go to a house across the street that belonged to a rich merchant named Kornilov. It was pleasantly free on the first morning; too free for the soldiers, especially those of the always hostile Second Regiment who (said Kobylinsky) had 'a very low moral standard'. The guard protested so noisily when it saw its prisoners crossing the road to visit the Kornilov house that Kobylinsky had to placate them by the erection of a wooden fence. This tall barrier went around the Governor's house and enclosed a side street, broad and little used, as a kind of muddy courtyard for exercise: the barracks for the guard overlooked it. Anyone from Kornilov's was allowed to cross unheeded; but traffic had to be strictly one-way.

Within a week or two the prisoners were as much at home as they could ever be. People in Tobolsk, many of them descendants of former exiles to Siberia, were warm and traditionally loyal; to them the Tsar remained the Tsar; they would watch, removing their hats and crossing themselves, for any member of the family to appear at a window. Some would kneel when Nicholas and Alexandra walked through a public garden, between ranks of soldiers, to early Mass. From the town and round about, regular gifts of food came to the house; nuns brought eggs and sugar. In spite of the recalcitrant guards—only a section of Kobylinsky's soldiers—life was reasonably serene and would have continued so if it had not been for an arrogant deputy commissar. Alexander Nikolsky arrived at the end of September with his chief, Vasily

67

Drawing by one of the Grand Duchesses of the Governor's House where they were confined in exile in Tobolsk. The church where they worshipped can be seen in the background.

Semenov Pankratov, to take over control: Kobylinsky, in charge of the troops, was subordinate to the newcomers. Pankratov, insignificant in appearance, was earnest, mild, and helpful: to Gilliard 'the typical enlightened fanatic'.* His friend Nikolsky was entirely different, a brutal type, stubborn and unkempt. Unlike Pankratov, he constantly sought revenge for his previous exile to Siberia as a social revolutionary. Thus – a relatively minor thing – he insisted that the prisoners must be photographed for identification as he had been long ago – full face and profile. 'It was forced on us in the old days. Now it's their turn.' Everyone

* When eighteen he had killed a gendarme in Kiev while defending a woman and had stayed in solitary confinement for fifteen years, after which he had another twenty-seven years of Siberian exile.

The view from the Governor's House. The house on the left, across the street, belonged to a rich merchant called Kornilov and provided lodgings for Gibbes and most of the Imperial suite.

thenceforth had to carry an identity card with a photograph and a number. Further, Nikolsky's influence and his extremist views began to affect the better-disposed soldiers: Pankratov was not blameless here, for his exposition of the miracles of Socialist-Revolutionary doctrine became perilously confused with Bolshevism.

This trouble apart, when Gibbes – 'Sydney Ivanovich' – entered Tobolsk at the beginning of October, life had moved into a fairly gentle rhythm, much as at Tsarskoe Selo and, on the whole, more congenial. The three younger Grand Duchesses and Alexis had their lessons; Alexandra read, embroidered, or painted; Nicholas walked in the compound, a poor substitute for the Imperial Park, or sawed his logs strenuously with anyone who would join him.

The Tsar and Gilliard sawing wood in the compound.

After tea at four o'clock they would stand at an upper window, or upon a balcony, and look at the random life of Tobolsk. Sometimes, after dinner, a few of them played cards. Alexis would go to bed at nine; everyone else at eleven. Kobylinsky openly admired the ex-Tsar's kindness, modesty, and knowledge, his lack of affectation, and his simple tastes in food and drink (such dishes as borshch or kasha, and a single glass of port or Madeira after dinner). He never minded what he wore; he enjoyed and needed physical labour. In a deposition at Ekaterinburg in the spring of 1919 Kobylinsky added charmingly: 'He did not understand art, but he liked nature and shooting. It was absolutely painful to him to abstain from shooting for any length of time, and he disliked any obligation to spend his time indoors.'

One of his failings was apparent: weakness of will. The ex-Tsar relied upon Alexandra, even in trivial details ('I will ask my wife; her wishes are mine'). Kobylinsky found Alexandra exceedingly reserved and always royal; she felt their position as captives far more than Nicholas did, and she had aged suddenly. According to Dr Botkin – though here Gibbes always disagreed – she suffered from hysteria in which her religious ecstasy had originated.

Gibbes, meantime, was on his tedious journey. At Tyumen he was just able to get the season's last river-boat before the isolation of the seven-months' Siberian winter closed in; isolation indeed, for when the Siberian railroad was driven across country so far to the south of Tobolsk, the little town was more or less abandoned to stagnate. On board the steamer he travelled along the broad, sluggish rivers until, round a curve, Tobolsk came into view, its often primitive buildings and its score of church cupolas set beneath the hill and overlooked by an old fortress (now law courts and prison), the cathedral, and the bishop's palace. Going straight to the Kornilov house, Gibbes encountered Pankratov who was polite and friendly. It seemed that he could not be admitted at once to the ex-Tsar; this was a matter the soldiers had to decide. Two days passed before the democratic rites were completed and the guard agreed that Gibbes could cross the road: a more important privilege than he thought at the time, for he was the last person admitted to the Imperial Family in Tobolsk. Pankratov allotted him a room in the Kornilov house. At length he was taken over to the family and, after a gap of seven months, a delighted welcome. Alexandra, facially much older and with many grey hairs, was sitting with Alexis in her upstairs

drawing-room as she often did when unwell or disinclined to go down to luncheon. Gibbes learnt that by now, and too late, she had begun to see that some of the people supposed to be devoted to her – Major General Ressin, for example, and Colonel Grabbe – had been merely time-servers. Nicholas, who had lunched with his suite, came upstairs immediately, glad to see a visitor from an outer world that was more and more cut off. 'But [said Gibbes] he absolutely pounced on me at first, for it was from English sources that he had received the severest blows. Attacks from revolutionary leaders in Russia he knew he must take and suffer, but those from England – to which he had been so loyal – had to be the unkindest of all.' He had never been so outspoken as he was that afternoon: a pale sun outside, townsfolk pattering by on the wooden pavements beneath, and the man who had been Autocrat of all the Russias reviewing his life in exile.

The Empress's drawing-room at Tobolsk.

Teaching at Tobolsk

Gibbes slipped at once into his old place. An expert teacher, he had never cared how many lessons he gave, and they meant more than ever in this confinement where every hour of the day had somehow to be filled. He had not been before at such close quarters with the whole Imperial Family. He noted the impressions which stayed with him through life, and which are here extracted from the more formal version that he gave to an examining magistrate in Ekaterinburg twenty months later. Briefly:

The ex-Tsar (Nicholas Alexandrovich): then fifty years old. Extremely honest, cheerful, kind, and compassionate, and a devoted lover of his country. He spoke and wrote English and French to perfection; his memory was exceptional. Preferring to study social matters and history, he did not worry about light reading. He was slightly reserved and disliked familiarity, though he sometimes chatted with the soldiers. Methodical in his habits, he could not bear anyone to touch his things.

The ex-Empress (Alexandra Fedorovna): then forty-five. Formerly very good-looking and graceful (her feet were large). She had wonderful soft grey eyes. She was clever, but appeared to be more so to those who knew her least. Not haughty in the ordinary sense, she never forgot her position; she looked queenly, but I was always at ease with her. Kind-hearted, extremely fond of homely secrets, she liked to prepare surprises. Russia she loved and considered herself a Russian, but she had German traits (and was more economical than an Englishwoman). Her genuinely religious feelings, in the Orthodox way, were quite normal and not induced by hysteria. Always a stronger, more aggressive character than the Tsar, she never opposed him; I never saw a single quarrel.

The Grand Duchess Olga Nicolaievna reached her twenty-second birthday at Tobolsk. Fair, with golden-brown hair, the lightest in the family, and beautiful blue eyes, she got much thinner after her illness [at Tsarskoe Selo]. She was innocent, modest, sincere, and kind, but easily irritated; her manners could be a little brusque. She liked

simplicity and paid little attention to dress. Her moral outlook reminded me of her father whom she loved better than anyone else. She was very religious.

The Grand Duchess Tatiana Nicolaievna, a tall, elegant girl, was then twenty; you could hardly find anyone so thin. She had a darker complexion than the others. Tatiana was haughty and reserved, dutiful and pensive; it was impossible to guess her thoughts, even if she was more decided in her opinions than her sisters. Though her technique as a pianist was better than the others, she showed no feeling when she played. She painted and embroidered well. I think the Empress preferred her to her sisters; any favour could be obtained only through Tatiana.

On the platform which the Tsar built on the roof of the greenhouse: Olga, Nicholas, Alexis, Tatiana, Marie, Anastasia.

Overprinted stamps collected by Alexis: 'they may be useful'.

The Grand Duchess Marie Nicolaievna, aged eighteen, was very strong and broadly-built and could easily lift me from the ground. Good-looking, with light grey eyes, she too grew very thin after her illness. She could paint and draw, and played the piano competently; less well than Olga or Tatiana. Marie was simple and fond of children; a little inclined to laziness; probably she would have made an excellent wife and mother. She liked Tobolsk and told me she could have made herself quite happy there.

The Grand Duchess Anastasia Nicolaievna, aged sixteen, was short and stout, the only ungraceful member of the family; she might have been the best looking had she been taller and slimmer. Her hair was lighter than Marie's, her eyes were grey and beautiful, her nose was straight. Refined and witty, she had all a comedienne's talent and made everyone laugh, without even laughing herself. It seemed as if her mental development had been suddenly arrested; and though she played the piano and painted, she was only in the first stages of either accomplishment.

The Tsarevich (Alexis Nicolaievich), aged thirteen, tall for his age and very thin, had suffered greatly in childhood from a disease inherited from his mother's family. He became worse in Tobolsk where treatment was hard to find. A clever boy, he was not fond of books. He had a kind heart – during the last Tobolsk days he was the only member of the family to give presents – and he loved animals. Influenced only through his emotions, he rarely did what he was told, but obeyed his father; his mother, loving him passionately, could not be firm with him, and through her he got most of his wishes granted. Alexis bore unpleasant things silently and without grumbling. He had some odd fancies. For example, at Tobolsk he used to collect old nails, saying 'They may be useful'.

Gibbes again had four members of the family – the three younger Grand Duchesses and Alexis – as his pupils. Through the years he preserved from Tobolsk two cheap exercise books, each labelled 'English'. 'M. Romanof' had written her name neatly on one label. The other book belonged to 'A. Romanova (Shut-Up!) Tobolsk 1917–1918.' Grand Duchess Anastasia, most exuberantly talkative of the sisters, seized on one of Gibbes's exasperated moments. When he told her to shut up, she asked him how to spell it and adopted it as her nickname. The sisters, using scratchy, spluttering pen-nibs, wrote uncommonly alike, a large laborious script with a heavy left-to-right slope. Their books, Anastasia's beginning in October, soon after Gibbes's arrival, they used for dictation and 'composition'. Marie was generally putting poems into prose. The chieftain of Ulva's isle

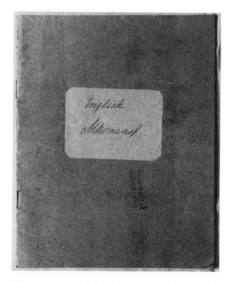

The cover of Marie's English exercise book.

promised a boatman 'lots of money' to row them over the water. Maud Muller, in Whittier's poem, married not the judge but a 'pesent' and had 'lots of children with which she occupied herself'. A gallant bride ensured that curfew should not ring that night. Browning supplied Hervé Riel ('all the French people have forgoten and don't speak any more about their herow'); and there was even the tale of the 'cane-bottomed chair', not the 'old armchair' of Eliza Cook.

Anastasia's writing is rather harder to read than her sister's. Among her subjects were 'the young knight Lochinvar who was very brave'; and King Robert of Sicily: 'He terned back and asked the priest who was sitting behind him what did those words mean. The clerk answered, "He has put down the mighty from their seat and has exalted them of low degree".' Three fishers were lost in the roaring 'waives'; men must work and women must weep. Mary called the cattle home. Evelyn Hope was 'lying in the cofen, very pretty.'

Suddenly, in the midst of the dictated paragraphs and of the prose renderings, plodding on with a charming naïveté, misspellings and all, and powdered with Gibbes's corrections, there occurs a single fragment of Anastasia's own experience. For a page or so, in the form of a letter to a friend, she was back on the train between Tsarskoe Selo and Tyumen. Gibbes went through it for her; but what Grand Duchess Anastasia wrote originally on a biting winter morning in Siberia was simply this:

My dear Friend. I will describe to you who [how] we travelled. We started in the morning and when we got into the train I went to sleap, so did all of us. We were very tierd because we did not sleap [had not slept] the whole night. The first day was hot and very dusty. At the stations we had to shut our window curtanse that nobody should see us. Once in the evening I was loking out of the window we stoped near a little house, but there was no staition so we could look out. A little boy came to my window and asked: "Uncle, please give me, if you have got, a newspaper." I said: "I am not an uncle but an anty and have no newspaper." At the first moment I could not understand why did he call me "Uncle" but then I rememberd that my hear is cut and I and the soldiers (which where standing next to me) laught very much. On the way many funy things had hapend, and if I shall have time I shall write to you our travell father on. Good by. Dont forget me. Many kisses from us all to you my darling. Your A.

The tale of 'The Cane-bottomed Chair' as told by Marie in her English exercise book, with Gibbes's corrections. Anastasia's English composition about their journey into exile is reproduced on the endpapers.

Siberian Winter

While the girls were accepting Gibbes's dictation, or fighting with English syntax, in a town where November's short grey days were merging into the hours of icy darkness, the Provisional Government of Russia had vanished for ever. It had been only a seven months' interregnum. Everywhere the Bolsheviks had prospered; and, in late August, Kornilov, Government Commander-in-Chief, resolved on a desperate coup, the despatch to Petrograd of a cavalry corps to rout the Soviet, and the formation of a military dictatorship which he would control (though Kerensky might have a Cabinet seat). Unwisely, the Socialist Kerensky, fearing this pressure from the Right, asked the Soviet to help him – a deal involving the release of Leon Trotsky and other prominent Bolsheviks. The rest followed with almost absurd ease. Kornilov's cavalry promptly made friends with the newly-formed Red Guards; these merely 'laught' – like Anastasia's soldiers – when asked by Kerensky to return the weapons they had been lent. The Bolsheviks secured a majority in the Petrograd Soviet; Lenin, still in Finland, sent another of his messages: 'History will not forgive us if we do not take power now.' Disguised, he was soon back in Petrograd during October – that thick-set little man with the small Tartar eyes and the round head – to hear the Bolshevik Central Committee, only two dissenting, vote for immediate insurrection. On the chosen day, 24 October/6 November, key points in Petrograd yielded practically without resistance while the life of the capital moved along much as usual. The cruiser *Aurora* had come up the Neva that morning and anchored off the Winter Palace; she was flying the red flag. Next day an open car drove from Petrograd, carrying a short, square-faced man with cropped hair and fiery eyes: Kerensky, making for the army in the south. In the early hours of 26 October/8 November the rump of the Provisional Government

surrendered; Kerensky, unsupported on his mission, hid for six months and ultimately escaped by way of Murmansk; during the rest of his fifty years he never saw Russia again:

The guard at Tobolsk under the Kerensky regime.

> Hardly a nation – half a continent:
> Old Europe with an older Asia blent.
> Why name the Tsars when we can celebrate
> The white-hot forging of a Workers' State?

Neither mail nor newspapers got through regularly to Tobolsk. It was unceasing anxiety for Nicholas, knowing only the rumours and little of the truth, as he sat day by day in his study with the portraits of Alexander II and the Tsarevich on the walls. Often he was reduced to reading what Gilliard described as 'a nasty local rag printed on packing-paper, which gave us only telegrams several days old and generally distorted and cut down'. When he did receive a large bundle of newspapers, with the rising in complete, even excessive detail, he was more shaken than Gibbes had ever known. This was the true Terror: was it for this he had abdicated? 'For the moment he was totally incapable of saying or doing anything, and no one dared to say a word. The mounting danger drew us all much closer together.'

Transiently, the Governor's House remained as it was. The

Bolshevik government had other tasks. 'Muslims of Russia,' it proclaimed,

Tartars of the Volga and Crimea, Kirghiz, Kazakhs and Sarts of Siberia and Turkestan, Turks and Tartars of Transcaucasia, Chechens and Mountaineers of the Caucasus, and all those whose mosques and oratories have been destroyed, whose beliefs and customs have been trampled under foot by the Tsars and oppressors of Russia. Your beliefs and usages, your natural and cultural institutions, are henceforth free and inviolate. Organise your life in complete freedom. You have the right. Know that your rights, like those of all the peoples of Russia, are under the powerful safeguard of the revolution and its organs, the Soviet of Workers, Soldiers, and Peasants. Lend your support to this revolution and its government.

Tobolsk, momentarily forgotten in its backlands, shivered under the glaze of winter. In spite of fires it could be frigid in the white building on Liberty Street where Alexandra sat making and mending for her family, and writing in a letter to Anna Vyrubova whom she had lost for ever: 'One lives from day to day . . . God have mercy and save Russia.' Outside ('Organise your life in complete freedom') Nicholas and the girls marched up and down the empty compound; Alexis, mercifully free from pain, played on skis or ran about collecting old nails and bits of string. Soldiers of the guard from the 2nd Regiment – seldom those from the 1st or 4th – could be boorishly obstructive, or Nikolsky, resolute as a mole, hunted round for a new minor tyranny. Earlier, when a case of wine arrived for Nicholas, sent from Petrograd with Kerensky's permission, Nikolsky had it thrown unopened into the river. Another case was brought in unseen. Suspicious, Nikolsky had the house searched room by room, not realising that the bottles had been thrust into a basket and that the man who carried it followed the searchers – always one room behind. So Nicholas did not lose his single glass for lunch and dinner, even if there was too little for anyone to join him.

At the turn of the year, in the full grip of winter, the family had to invent some way of entertaining itself through the bleak evenings. It was simpler by day. All could persuade themselves then, a trifle feverishly, that they had to keep to an essential routine. The girls and Alexis would have three or four hours of lessons: Grand Duchesss Olga, too old for school, suffered more from ennui than the others did, though she did begin to teach German to Tatiana. There were protracted walks, steady tramping over the same old patch of snow. Nicholas, determined to get as much exercise as he could, built a platform on the roof of the orangery (or greenhouse). The other men helped him to make steps up to it; and Nicholas, who dreaded nothing more than a life indoors, liked to sit out there. On most late afternoons the Tsarevich would ask for one of his favourite card games, 'The slower you ride the farther you go' (or less haste, more speed), played as a rule by Alexis himself with either Gilliard or Gibbes on one side; and Prince Dolgoruky and Mlle Schneider on the other. At the end of nearly every game Schneider, who treated it all too seriously, would swear that this must be the last time. Alexis did not like to lose; he would merely become very silent and go into the next game with concentrated fervour.

These things took care of the day. Evening was the problem. After dinner the family would assemble in the big downstairs room, the only really comfortable room in the house. Frequently Nicholas would read aloud; Alexandra would have a few games of bezique with General Tatishchev or else work in her chair; the Grand Duchesses bent over their needlework. Dull enough; but Gibbes proposed another way of filling the hours. Why not perform plays on Sunday nights and rehearse them during the week? Here he could be an actor again – an instinct he had never lost – and a producer into the bargain. Among his books he had a clutch of short English sketches; Gilliard contributed a few in French; and, as a gala production, there was Anton Chekhov's one-act piece, *The Bear,* a farce (suggested by a Russian version of a French 'vaudeville') that nearly thirty years before had been a triumph in Moscow and St Petersburg. Its three characters are 'a landowning, dimpled little widow', a middle-aged landowner, and an aged footman. Popova, the widow, for seven months in deep mourning, is as resolutely sad as Shakespeare's Olivia after her brother's death. Her husband owed money to Smirnov, who calls gruffly for its repayment; being, she says, in 'a state of mind', she refuses until her steward returns. Smirnov explodes, first in a sequence of angry monologues, then before Popova herself when the argument shifts from money to the nature of women (a furious harangue) and to a noisy free-for-all in which even the footman is enmeshed. Smirnov challenges her to shoot it out. ('If she fights, well that's equality of rights, emancipation and all that Here

The Tsar's study.

The snowy compound of the Governor's House provided an exercise ground.

the sexes are equal! I'll shoot her on principle!') Inevitably, a richly farcical last scene ends in a prolonged kiss. This went splendidly in the crowded Tobolsk room, with Nicholas (the only part he played) managing to work himself into Smirnov's rages, Olga as Popova, and Marie filling in.

Other plays, for which Nicholas and Alexandra would write out formal programmes, were less exacting. Gibbes had some featherweight farcical sketches, one of them Leopold Montague's *The Crystal-Gazer* from the late 1890s. Owing to bad staff-work a bogus seer mixes his clients; hence a good deal of cross-purposes comedy about a lost lover who is actually a lost dog. 'The fact is,' says the seer haughtily, 'I mistook you for another person. If you insist on calling without a proper appointment, it is no fault of mine if you have to put up with a vision intended for somebody else.' And so on. Gibbes, as the crystal-gazer

Olga and Alexis.

In the dining-room in the Governor's House: left to right, Olga, General Tatishchev, Gilliard, Countess Hendrikov, Tatiana, Mlle Schneider.

(a woman in the original) acted with Grand Duchess Marie; and the family's dog Shot looked in as the lost poodle. Alexandra, who went backstage afterwards to examine the make-up, thought esoterically that Gibbes in a long white beard reminded her of a former Bishop of Wakefield. Tatiana partnered Gibbes in H. V. Esmond's gentle trifle from 1896, *In and Out of a Punt*.

Probably the cast had its happiest night with an Edwardian farcical sketch by Harry Grattan, called *Packing Up*: vulgar, said Gibbes, and exceedingly funny. Anastasia had the principal male part, Marie was the wife, and Alexis (with only a few lines) a porter: it was the sole Tobolsk production to have a consecutive run of two performances.

At the end of the farce [Gibbes reported] the husband has to turn his back, open his dressing-gown as if to take it off – Anastasia wore an old one of mine – and then exclaim: 'But I've packed my trousers; I can't go.' The night's applause had excited the little Grand Duchess. The piece had gone with a swing and they were getting through the 'business' so fast that a draught got under the gown and whisked its tail up to the middle of her back, showing her sturdy legs and bottom encased in the Emperor's Jaeger underwear. We all gasped; Emperor and Empress, suite and servants, collapsed in uncontrolled

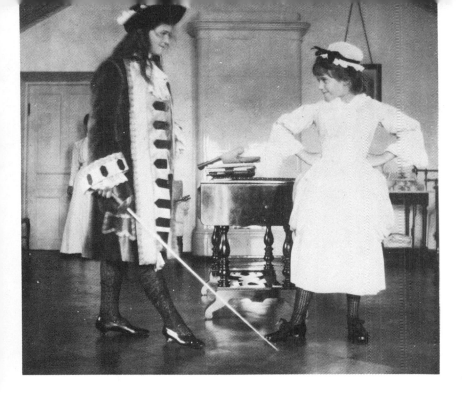

laughter. Poor Anastasia could not make it out. All were calling for a second performance, but this time she was more careful. Certainly I shall always remember the night; it was the last hearty unrestrained laughter the Empress ever enjoyed.

Pierre Gilliard did his share by providing a brief French sketch, *Accident de bicyclette,* about a collision between a Frenchman and an Englishman, and the Englishman's discomfiture, somewhere in the Bois de Boulogne. During the early spring of 1918, when conditions were far worse, Gibbes had been meaning to do W. A. Mackersy's duologue, *Rats,* but before anything could happen the calendar had moved into Lent: all plays abandoned and Alexis exasperated: he had learned most of his part and enjoyed it. 'On the first four days of Lent,' Gibbes said, 'the wonderful Canon of St Andrew of Crete was read, and with her usual thoroughness the Empress provided a copy of the Canon, in Russian, for everyone present.'

Every book in the house was read over and over. Gibbes had several with him, in particular John Richard Green's *A Short History of the English People*:

I took it to Tobolsk as I expected to be put in prison, and thought that if I were, it would be a good book to read. In

The room where the four Grand Duchesses slept. This photograph shows Anastasia's, Marie's and Tatiana's beds. Olga's is off the picture to the right.

Tobolsk the Emperor told me that his favourite subject was history and asked me whether I had no serious book that I could lend him. Previously I had lent him and the others many light romantic works.

84

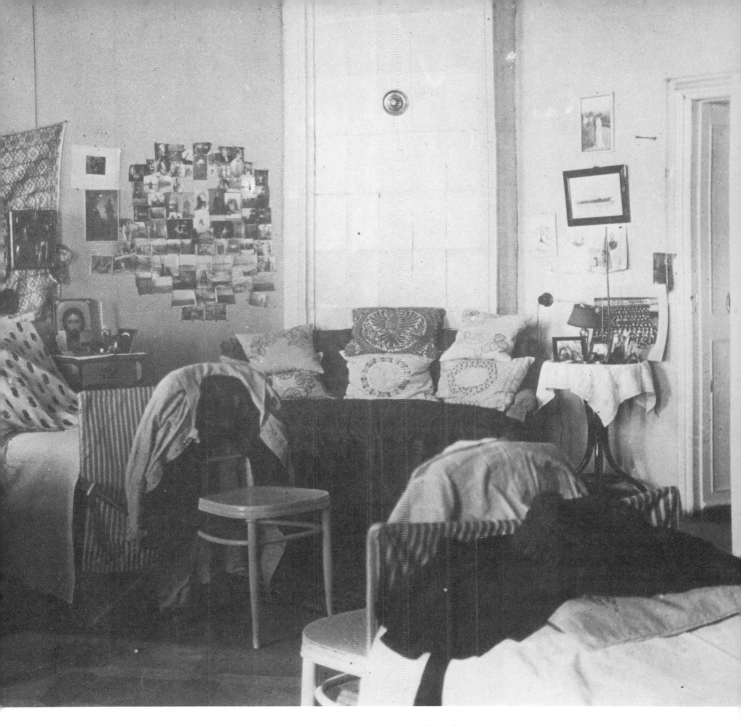

I gave him Green at once; and he read it, cover to cover, in the
two hours after breakfast and before the mid-morning recreation at
eleven in which all the children joined. He was reading this book at

Winter in Tobolsk.

the end of 1917 and the beginning of 1918 and said that he had much enjoyed it; he had read most of these subjects when he was young, but had no time for it later. I very much wanted him to write an appreciation on the fly-leaf, but I was too shy to [ask him] do so.

Gibbes kept the book wrapped up in a copy of the *Journal des débats*, the French newspaper which should have been received daily and seldom was. The Imperial Family's other papers, when they came, were *The Times*—which Nicholas said they had taken as long as he could remember—and *The Daily Graphic*: this, Gibbes believed, was the only one of the three ever read.

Among the lighter books he lent to the family were novels by R. W. Chambers (*The Maid at Arms*), L. Allen Harker (*Mr Wycherley's Wards*), Hall Caine (*The White Prophet*), Stanley Weyman (*Under the Red Robe*) and W. J. Locke (*The White Dove* and *Idols*). They had Scott's *Quentin Durward*, Thackeray's *Vanity Fair*, and Ainsworth's *Old St Paul's*; animal stories, *The Biography of a Silver Fox* and *Monarch: The Big Bear of Tallac*, by Ernest Thompson Seton; and, extraordinary in these surroundings, Talbot Baines Reed's late Victorian school story, *The Fifth Form at St Dominic's*. Besides a selected and abridged Shakespeare, there was a single text of *As You Like It*. Alexis loved Rider Haggard's *King Solomon's Mines*, which Gibbes was reading to him soon after coming to Tobolsk and had to repeat; Conan Doyle's *Memoirs of Sherlock Holmes*—the volume that ends with the last struggle between Holmes and Moriarty at the Reichenbach Falls—and Sir Samuel Baker's *Cast Up by the Sea*. ('As I read this book the Tsarevich became very fond of it: he took a great interest in Ned, and when the book was finished, he wanted it again. I was reading it during the February Revolution when the Empress sometimes sat with us; the Tsarevich was then sick in bed.') Gibbes had also copies of stories retold for children: *Ivanhoe, Dombey and Son, David Copperfield,* and *The Tower of London* which, in this order of preference, Alexis listened to when he was ill. Tatiana and Anastasia also got through *Ivanhoe.* One of several schoolbooks, Nesfield's *Junior Course of English Composition,* was inscribed on the fly-leaf: 'Olga. 19/11/09g. Tsarskoe Selo. Thursday.' 'Olga' was written in English; the letter 'g' after the date stood for *goda* (year); 'Tsarskoe Selo' was written in Russian, and 'Thursday' in English, the day of the week in November 1909 when Gibbes used the *Junior Course* at the beginning of his second year's work. That was a period from the other side of the gulf when no one breathed the word 'revolution'. Later the idea crept gradually into common talk until Gibbes was astonished to hear people who had everything to lose from a revolution playing with the idea intellectually. Then, swift and crushing, it happened, like the sudden death of a person who had lain sick for so many years that somehow the end was unbelievable. It had become amply believable by the time that the captives waited in the strange dulling claustrophobia of Tobolsk. A prayer in verse exists, composed, it is thought, by Countess Hendrikov, transcribed by Grand Duchess Olga, and copied by Gibbes in this English version:

Grant us thy patience, Lord,
In these our woeful days,
The mob's wrath to endure,
The torturers' ire;

Thy unction to forgive
Our neighbours' persecution,
And mild, like Thee, to bear
A bloodstained Cross.

And when the mob prevails,
And foes come to despoil us,
To suffer humbly shame,
O Saviour aid us!

And when the hour comes
To pass the last dread gate,
Breathe strength in us to pray,
Father, forgive them!

Prayers given by the Empress to Gibbes, Christmas, 1917:
I pray
That Christ the Xmas King may stoop to bless,
And guide you day by day to holiness,
Your Friend in joy, your Comfort in distress;
I pray
That every cloud may lead you to the light,
And He may raise you up from height to height,
Himself the Day-Star of your darkest night;
I pray
That Christ, before whose Crib you bend the knee,
May fill your longing soul abundantly,
With grace to follow Him more perfectly.
1917
Tobolsk   Alexandra

Letter to Miss Jackson

In the ebb of the year the rigours of imprisonment had grown. There had been extremely hazy, chimerical notions of escape: ideas comforting for a while in theory, in practice almost impossible, though various monarchist groups were at work without any sure plans and in vain and needless rivalry. Much appeared to focus on a man named Boris Soloviev, who worked from Tyumen; a dubious soldier-of-fortune who commended himself to Alexandra because he was the son-in-law of Rasputin. His complex cloak-and-dagger games proved to be utterly useless. He might well have been a double agent working for both the Bolsheviks (betraying loyal monarchist officers) and the Germans. Soloviev came from a dim underworld; his machinations did nothing whatever for the Imperial Family which was used by now to the sting of hope deferred.

Within the Governor's House Gibbes wrote during December a letter to a Miss Margaret Jackson, who lived in London at a home for governesses in Regent's Park. This letter he sent to Petrograd, hoping it would be passed on in the diplomatic bag. More than thirty years before, in Hesse-Darmstadt, Margaret Jackson had taught Princess Alix of Hesse, later Empress Alexandra, who knew her as 'Madgie' and who responded to her interest in politics. They had always corresponded; but now, surprisingly, it was Sydney Gibbes who wrote. He composed the letter carefully. Among his papers he kept two or three texts, corrected drafts and the final document:

Dear Miss Jackson,
   You will have read in the newspapers of the many different changes that have taken place. In August the Provisional Government decided to change the residence from Tsarskoé to Tobolsk, a small town far away in Siberia, 300 versts from the nearest railway station. The change has now been effected, and we are established in our quarters,

88

From a family group taken in July 1878. Princess Alix (later Empress Alexandra of Russia) is the small girl sitting on the step of the carriage. Her parents are behind her and her governess, Miss Margaret Jackson ('Madgie') is at the back in a black hat (Reproduced by gracious permission of Her Majesty the Queen).

the residence of the former Governor. The town itself is perhaps better than one might expect, but it is nevertheless extremely primitive. It is grouped round the foot of a steep hill leading on to a high plateau on which are situated the principal cathedral, containing the local shrine, the Bishop's palace, and a great building now used as the Assize Courts. Although the town contains but 25,000 inhabitants, there are more than twenty churches, and their spires and towers, often of quaint and curious design, give the town a light and pleasant aspect. By custom the churches are generally washed white and the roof painted a pale green, being sometimes further embellished with a tiny cupola and cross of burnished gold, and against the clear pale blue sky they make a charming picture as they sparkle in the brilliant northern sunshine.

Our House, or rather Houses, for there are two, one on one side of the street and one on the other, are the best in the town; that in which the Household proper lives is entirely isolated and possesses a small garden besides a piece of the roadway which has been railed in

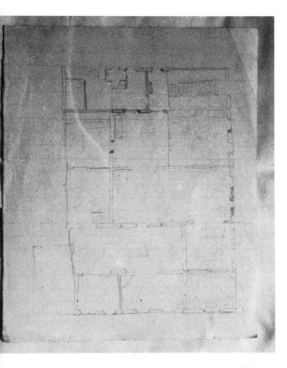

Sketch plan of the Governor's House kept with Gibbes's drafts of the letter to Miss Jackson. Was it a concealed cry for help?

to make a recreation ground. The other house which is almost exactly opposite, is occupied by Government officials and contains quarters for the Suite. The House itself is not very large, but the rooms are pleasant and bright. As in almost all Russian houses, on mounting the principal staircase you enter the saloon on one side of which is the study and on the other the drawing-room. After these come the principal bedroom and a room which the four daughters use as a dormitory. The latter is bright and cosy with its four camp beds round which are arranged the most treasured possessions of each. The youngest has a room to himself on the other side of the corridor that serves him for bedroom and classroom too. The dining-room is downstairs, being more conveniently situated to the kitchens. The days do not vary much except for Sundays and Holidays and their Eves when there are prayers read by a benign old priest in whose parish we live. On Sunday we are generally permitted to go to the Parish Church to the Communion Service, but otherwise prayers are read at home. The Services are very nice and sympathetically performed and there is now a small choir which sings really well. The younger members of the family have lessons in the morning before lunch, after which we all take exercise and recreation in our small railed-in plot. It is difficult to obtain much variety in so small a space; walking and sawing wood and similar occupations help to pass the time and afford the exercise necessary for health. Fortunately all keep well and in good spirits in spite of the times through which we live. Of the outside world we only know what we can gather from the newspapers which in this remote spot come slowly and at irregular intervals.

It is ages since you wrote, or maybe your letters have not arrived! Try and write again, perhaps the next will reach its destination. Send news of everybody, how they are and what they are doing. I hear that David is back from France, how are his father and mother? And the cousins, are they also at the Front?

It has now turned very cold and the ground is covered with snow, but for this region the cold has set in remarkably late and the autumn was quite magnificently fine. Until a week ago it was very dark in the morning, especially when we made our way to church through the deserted Town Garden, but now that the clock has been put back an hour it is already quite light before we set out. In the dark with sentries at every few yards, with a raw and biting cold wind, the effect was a little awesome and depressing. But it is nice to be able to go, for the service is very comforting. The same priest officiates, but he is assisted by a deacon as well as the choir, the whole being reverently and harmoniously performed. It lasts little more than an hour when the procession is re-formed and wends its way back much in the order in which it came, by the light of the newly-risen sun.

Superficially, a harmless descriptive letter. But why should Gibbes have troubled to write at this length to Miss Jackson, to him an unknown figure except for a professional bond? The last paragraph but one is the clue: 'I hear that David is back from France, how are his father and mother . . .?' David was his family's name for the Prince of Wales. Clearly then the letter, which also contains a very rough plan of the Governor's House at Tobolsk, was principally from Alexandra – some of the phrasing suggests this – and intended to reach King George and Queen Mary by way of Miss Jackson: a concealed cry for help.

No answer arrived. Gibbes was worried, for seventeen months later he wrote (to an unnamed London official) from Vladivostok, a letter of which simply this partial draft remains:

The British High Commission, Vladivostok.
1st May 1919.

Sir,

While in Tobolsk whither I had accompanied the late Imperial Family, at the Empress's request I wrote a letter addressed to a Miss Jackson but intended for the King and Queen. It was not then possible for them or indeed for me to communicate with the outside world except under strict censorship, and for reasons which I am sure you would appreciate, the Empress could not write personally. In these circumstances the Empress did me the honour to avail herself of my services, and though I was personally unknown to Miss Jackson, I wrote her a letter in which I endeavoured to acquaint her with these and other circumstances of our life which I was desired to send.

We were sure that a letter written by myself to a compatriot in England would pass out of the house without arousing suspicion, and indeed I heard later of its safe arrival in Petrograd. The letter was sent from Tobolsk on December 15th, 1917, and sent on from Petrograd by bag, addressed to Miss Jackson at a Home for Governesses in Regent's Park, London. The Empress was sure that Miss Jackson would carry the letter to the Queen but I have had no means of finding out whether it really reached its destination and I am now writing to you that enquiry may be made should it have miscarried.

That is all. The letter does not appear to have been preserved in the Royal Archives at Windsor; but there are other documents there, relating to Gibbes, which seem to indicate that the Royal Family was interested in him and in any information about the Imperial captives.

Draft of a later letter from Gibbes. 'The Empress was sure Miss Jackson would carry the letter to the Queen.'

Destination Unknown

In spite of everything Kobylinsky could do, disaffected soldiers of the Tobolsk guard were progressively more truculent. Angered by poor food and unfulfilled promises of better pay, they turned their wrath against prisoners who lived in relative luxury. On an unfortunate Christmas Day the family went to early Mass. After it, imprudently, the deacon – by order of the 'benign old priest' of Gibbes's letter – intoned the once customary Thanksgiving Prayer omitted after the abdication. Several soldiers were in church. At the close of the service, which Kobylinsky himself had not heard in full, Pankratov came to him in alarm: 'Do you know what Father Vasiliev has done? He has read the prayer for the long life of the Emperor, the Empress, and the whole family, mentioning their names. As soon as the soldiers heard it they began to murmur.' It was more than a murmur, almost a riot. The clergy's lives were endangered until the local bishop transferred Vasiliev to a monastery and appointed another priest. Unsatisfied, the Soldiers' Committee withdrew the family's privilege of churchgoing, except on important Holy Days in the Orthodox Calendar; they ordered, too, that a soldier should always be present at any service in the Governor's House: a hated infliction. Presently Bolsheviks in the guard took control; the Committee dismissed Pankratov – the 'little man' as Nicholas would call him – and his friend Nikolsky as well. There had been various ignorant decisions. The household had put up in the compound an ice hill that greatly amused the Grand Duchesses and Alexis. First, the soldiers objected to any playing on it that could be seen from the street. When a party from the reasonably tractable Fourth Regiment was leaving Tobolsk, Nicholas and Alexandra climbed the hill to say good-bye. At once the remaining troops, including some politically-minded newcomers, 'a pack of blackguardly-looking young men', said Gilliard, razed the hill to

the ground on the score that if any member of the Imperial
Family was shot while on it, the soldiers would be blamed. At
another time Nicholas, who had put on a Caucasian tribal dress
to go to a party given by Gibbes, wore a dagger in his belt.
Promptly the guard proclaimed a search for weapons: Nicholas
had to surrender his dagger, and Dolgoruky and Gilliard their
sabres.

In its death-pangs the Provisonal Government had forgotten
any obligation to keep the Tobolsk household. Somewhere
Kobylinsky had to find credit, and ultimately he managed to raise
a loan of 20,000 roubles from a monarchist merchant. While he
was dealing with such a problem as this – it was 'hell, not life', he
said – his soldiers, ingenious with petty humiliations, devised a
new one. Officers must remove their shoulder-straps; Nicholas,
who wore a colonel's shoulder-straps on his khaki shirt, would
be included. In fact, the Committee's spokesman warned
Kobylinsky that if the ex-Tsar refused to obey, he would tear off
the straps himself. No argument could be heard: Nicholas wore
thenceforth a black sheepskin overcoat, unbadged. Next, the
Bolsheviks at the centre, suddenly recollecting Tobolsk, telegraphed
from Petrograd that in future the Imperial family must receive

*Liberty Street. The church where the
Imperial Family worshipped can be
seen in the distance.*

An altar set up in the Governor's House when the Imperial Family was forbidden to go out to church. The Empress's bedspread serves as an altar-cloth.

only soldiers' rations, quarters, and heating; no person must spend more than 150 roubles a week. To comply, the family had to make rigid economies. A dozen servants were discharged, and food was reduced to only two courses at a meal: soup and meat: no butter, cream, or coffee.

At the beginning of April, a fresh order. Everyone had to leave the Kornilov house and to come under guard with the family. The sole exceptions were Gibbes, allowed to have a small neighbouring room, and the doctors Derevenko and Botkin. Overcrowding was serious, though Kobylinsky contrived to keep the family inviolate. Baroness Buxhoeveden, who had asked to join Alexandra, was refused admission and searched humiliatingly; she had to lodge in the town.

News from the centre was catastrophic. Lenin – who had moved the capital from Petrograd to Moscow – needed peace to shape his new Russia. The army, told that the war would end, was disarrayed. Planning only for the moment, desperate for a breathing-space, a *peredyshka,* Lenin agreed to Germany's savage demands: an ultimatum had practically expired when at last he carried his colleagues with him. German headquarters of the Eastern Front were at Brest-Litovsk, and there, on 18 February/3 March, the Bolsheviks signed away four thousand square miles of territory: Finland, Esthonia, Livonia, Courland, Lithuania, Russian Poland. When the bare details crept into Tobolsk, Nicholas was stricken. The Bolsheviks, aware now that Germany would be glad to capture the ex-Tsar as a Russian symbol to fortify the Treaty, resolved to take him from the old 'Kerensky rule' and put him under firmer restraint. There were frightening developments. The fanatical regional Soviet of the long-rebellious mining town of Ekaterinburg in the Urals was impatient to grab the Imperial Family. It sent its demand to Moscow – and indeed an Ekaterinburg party travelled to Tobolsk – but, before any answer came, a Bolshevik force from the rival city of Omsk also reached Tobolsk to dissolve the local government and impose the new order. For more than a week Omsk and Ekaterinburg waited to seize the family; but still the Central Executive Committee had not spoken. It was then that a new Commissar, from Moscow itself, drove authoritatively into the town on 9/22 April. He was not Leon Trotsky, as some had rumoured, but Vasily Vaslevich Yakovlev, a muscular man, tall and thin with jet-black hair, who dressed like a sailor but who seemed to be educated. In supreme command, he tried to

A service in an improvised chapel in the ballroom, with the priest officiating and nuns acting as choir.

placate the soldiers by telling them that they would get an extra three roubles daily and at once.

At Yakovlev's coming Alexis was gravely ill. After a good winter he had been putting much of his energy into new games. In trying to ride down the inside stairs of the Governor's house upon a boat with runners that he had used out on the ice hill, he had an awkward fall. The ensuing haemorrhage – bleeding into the groin – which Gilliard said was worse than anything at Spala, brought intolerable agony. The right foot was paralysed. He was heard to cry: 'I would like to die, Mama; I'm not afraid of death, but I'm so afraid of what they may do to us here.' Gibbes was sitting by him when Nicholas, with Yakovlev and another man, entered the room and Nicholas said: 'This is my son, and this gentleman is his tutor.'

Within three days Yakovlev told Kobylinsky that, under orders, he was going to take Nicholas from Tobolsk – he did not say where. Because the boy was ill the family could wait. A little later on 12/25 April Gibbes was again with the Tsarevich whose

A revolutionary procession passing the Governor's House.

mother had promised to come back after lunch. He called 'Mama! Mama!' but there was no answer; Gibbes, going out to look, saw Nicholas, Alexandra and Yakovlev in the middle of the hall. Flatly Nicholas had refused to go. Whereupon Yakovlev had told him he could take any others he wished; they would start at four next morning. Externally calm, though her eyes were red, Alexandra

came in to Alexis; she whispered to Gibbes that her husband had been ordered to leave Tobolsk, that she and Marie would accompany him, and that as soon as Alexis was better the rest would follow. She and Nicholas dined upstairs alone. Afterwards everyone gathered for tea in Alexandra's room with its beautiful water-colours. Composed once more – she had been praying with

Alexis – she sat quiet upon the sofa. Besides Marie (whom her sisters called 'Mashka') those going on the unknown journey were Prince Dolgoruky, Marshal of the Imperial Court; Dr Botkin, Court physician; Nicholas's valet, Alexandra's lady's maid, a cook, and a footman. The maid, Anna Stepanovna Demidova, was in pitiable terror. 'I am so frightened of the Bolsheviks, Mr Gibbes,' she said; 'I don't know what they will do to us.' 'It was [wrote Gibbes] the most mournful and depressing party I ever attended. There was not much talking and no pretence at gaiety. It was solemn, tragic, a fit prelude to inescapable catastrophe. After the party the suite went below and just sat and waited about.'

In the flaking darkness immediately before day, horses clopped into the courtyard of the Governor's House. They were drawing, for the arduous journey to Tyumen, what could be hardly more than bare peasant carts, unsprung and unseated, *tarantasses* as they were known, like large wicker baskets slung from two flexible poles. Only one of them had a hood. Hastily, members of the household gathered up what wisps of straw they could find in the back-yard for the floors; in the hooded cart they placed a mattress for Alexandra. Yakovlev helped her into Botkin's fur overcoat and had another coat brought out for the doctor. In the glass porch, by the light of the stars, Nicholas and Alexandra made their farewells. 'He had a handshake and a word for everyone,' Gibbes said, 'and we all kissed the Empress's hand.' Nicholas had to ride with Yakovlev in the open cart; Marie sat with her mother. Within minutes the sad little procession, flanked by its cavalry escort, creaked and jingled away from Tobolsk in the cold greyness of dawn. Behind, the three Grand Duchesses went in tears to their room; for a long time Alexis had been weeping.

A frightful journey to Tyumen involved the crossing of the Irtysh on melting ice, water up to the horses' chests, and afterwards a passage on foot across the Tobol where the ice was more dangerous still. Horses were changed several times. Well before Tyumen, Red cavalry met the carts for the final fourteen miles. At the station while Yakovlev telegraphed to Moscow – which, as Nicholas had guessed, was to have been their goal – the captives were transferred to a special train. This was waiting to leave when Yakovlev, on his own account, decided that instead of using the direct Moscow route – and being in peril of capture by the Ural Regional Soviet at Ekaterinburg – it would be wiser to go on a roundabout journey by way of Omsk.

It was too late. Once the train had left Tyumen, Ekaterinburg was warned; the Ural Soviet denounced Yakovlev and passed on a message to the West Siberian Soviet in Omsk, warning it to halt the Imperial party. Sixty miles from Omsk, troops blocked the line. Yakovlev, leaving his party to wait, took the engine and a single coach into the town and again got in touch with Moscow. Thence Jacob Sverdlov, who was Chairman of the Executive Committee of the All-Russian Congress of Soviets, told him without emotion that there was no hope; he would have to hand his prisoners over to the comrades at Ekaterinburg. In short, a death sentence.

Hours later, in Ekaterinburg station where the mob was crying 'Show us the Romanovs!' the Regional Soviet took formal charge of Nicholas and Alexandra. (Prince Dolgoruky was removed at once to prison and was never seen again.) The ex-Tsar had said he would rather go anywhere than the hostile Urals; here he was in their midst. That night, greeted at the door with the contemptuous words, 'Citizen Romanov, you may enter,' he slept in the house of Ipatiev with its sinister designation, 'The House of Special Purpose'. They had been stringently searched. Pathetically, in their bedroom Alexandra scribbled a good-luck swastika and added the date: 17/30 April, 1918. Meanwhile, the Chairman of the Ural Soviet was signing a receipt:

Prince Dolgoruky.

THE WORKMEN AND PEASANTS' GOVERNMENT OF THE RUSSIAN FEDERATIVE REPUBLIC OF SOVIETS
Ural District Soviet of the Workmen,
Peasants' and Soldiers' Deputies Presidio
EKATERINBURG, *April 30, 1918**

On the 30th of April, 1918, I, the undersigned, Chairman of the Ural District Soviet of Workmen's, Peasants' and Soldiers' Deputies, Alexander Georgevich Beloborodov, received from the Commissar of the All-Russian Central Executive Committee, Vasily Vaslevich Yakovlev, the following persons transferred from the town of Tobolsk: (1) the former Tsar, Nicholas Alexandrovich Romanov; (2) former Tsaritsa, Alexandra Fedorovna Romanova; (3) former Grand Duchess, Marie Nicolaievna Romanova—all of them to be kept under guard in the Town of Ekaterinburg.

(*Signed*) A. BELOBORODOV.
Member of District Executive Committee,
(*Signed*) D. DIDKOVSKY.

* New style.

99

The Last Journey

It was a most wearing period at Tobolsk; for days no definite news except a telegram from Tyumen. But presently a letter, dictated by Alexandra, advised the Grand Duchesses to 'dispose of the medicines as agreed'; and for several days the girls, supervised by Tatiana, more naturally a leader than Olga (always retiring), steadily sewed jewels into their clothing, inside hats and bodices, buttons and corsets. The Bolsheviks had removed Kobylinsky from command; Red Guards arrived from Ekaterinburg under a Commissar named Rodionov, a vicious man of about thirty, who was ordered to bring on the rest of the family as soon as Alexis, who remained exceedingly ill, could travel. Rodionov insisted on a daily roll-call for the prisoners; he refused to let the Grand Duchesses lock their door at night. Alexis, unable to be moved, lay in bed in his father's study while Gibbes or Gilliard read to him. Gibbes had begun Fenimore Cooper's *The Pathfinder*, brought from the children's bookcase at Tsarskoe Selo and inscribed on the title-page in Russian, probably in the Dowager Empress Marie's handwriting, 'Olga, from Grandmother on Christmas tree at Gachina, 1907'. On a sheet of thick paper Gibbes made some illustrative drawings, the clearest of them an Indian canoe; the paper came from a box that had once held sweets and then the cards of the 'Slower-you-ride-the-farther-you-go' that had been the Tsarevich's favourite game.

Gibbes kept these drawings. He preserved, too, some of the menus that, at all times, had been written out formally, day by day, in elaborate script on paper headed by the Imperial crest. Among the meals during the interregnum after Nicholas, Alexandra and Marie had left Tobolsk, were these (it must be remembered that description and food could be leagues apart):

Menu for the last day at Tobolsk. Lunch : borshch, hazel-hen (a sort of partridge) with rice ; dinner : veal garnished and macaroni.

Alexis was too ill to be moved and lay in bed in his father's study. His sisters are taking tea with him (from a faded photograph in Gibbes's album).

22 April/5 May 1918 :
    Lunch : Broth with root vegetables
      Cold meat
    Dinner : Cold ham
      Hot turkey
      Salad
23 April/6 May
    Lunch : Fresh shchi [cabbage soup]
      Escalope of veal, garnished
    Dinner : Galantine of turkey
      Hot wild duck
28 April/11 May
    Lunch : Russian soup with pearl barley
      Grouse with rice
    Dinner : Hot wild duck
      Salad
      Rice pudding
29 April/12 May
    Lunch : Borshch
      Veal rissoles, garnished
    Dinner : Leg of veal, garnished
      Macaroni

Eventually, by 6/19 May, Alexis could travel, though he could no longer walk. Departure was fixed for next day.

It was only on this last evening [Gibbes wrote] that we called for the two remaining bottles of wine [once again it was 'veal garnished

Alexis sitting up in bed (from a faded photograph).

and macaroni']. It was impossible to take them away, and it was agreed that the next best thing to do was to drink them. While we were doing so the new Commandant★ was heard sneaking down the corridor. We had only just time to hide the bottles and our glasses under the table, concealed by a long trailing cloth, when in he walked. He stood by the door, giving a quizzical look all round, and immediately we felt like little schoolboys caught doing something naughty at school. The situation was so ludicrous that as our eyes met we could contain ourselves no longer, but burst into a wild yell of uncontrollable laughter. The Commandant, more mystified than ever, did not know what to make of it, but as laughter is not generally a concomitant of plotting, he left it at that and went away.

Next day, at noon, his inseparable sailor-companion Nagorny – once partner of the disloyal Derevenko – carried the crippled Tsarevich from the river-wharf to the steamer *Rus*, remembered from the previous summer. But now Rodionov, who was in charge of an evil-looking detachment, insisted on padlocking Alexis and

★ Tatishchev, who had been attached to the Russian Embassy in Berlin, thought he remembered having seen Rodionov there; the man said nothing but admitted later that he had served as a spy on Russian revolutionaries. Gibbes recalled that in 1916, 'when in Petrograd at the home of a Jewish friend, a Russian citizen who worked in a cable factory, I asked him where he had been. He told me he had been to visit someone whose name I have forgotten. "Probably a German spy," he said; and he told me that an officer called Rodionov had been there too.'

Permit for Gibbes to leave Tobolsk.

Nagorny into their cabin, even though it was made clear that at any time the child might need a doctor. The girls, on the other hand, were forbidden to lock their cabin door.

Alexis and Olga on board the Rus *at the beginning of their last journey.*

Gibbes was with the family, and Baroness Buxhoeveden had been allowed to join them. Upon reaching Tyumen the *Rus* was moored to the bank opposite a waiting train. In hats and coats, passengers waited in the main saloon until Comrade Rodionov entered with a list from which he began to read. First, he named members of the Imperial suite and certain of the servants, and these rose and left. The Imperial children, summoned next, walked slowly up the bank, Nagorny bearing Alexis. Rodionov re-entered. 'The rest of you!' he said curtly. When Gibbes, Gilliard, and their companions got to the train they were put in the fourth class, a heated goods wagon (*teplushka*) and cut off completely from the Grand Duchesses and the Tsarevich who were in an ordinary passenger coach. Gibbes realised later that there had been no chance to say good-bye.

After midnight on 10/23 May the train clattered into the outskirts of Ekaterinburg. It stopped briefly at the principal station, just long enough for Rodionov to get out and make his report.

Then, the night long [said Gibbes], we kept moving backwards and forwards, halting for a short time in some inaccessible place in order

The gangway where the Rus *docked at Tyumen.*

to change our direction. Finally, about seven o'clock in the morning, the stop seemed to be more prolonged, I peered into the drizzle. We were standing in a detached spot where some local droshkies were waiting at the side of the line. Soon I saw the three Grand Duchesses, Olga, Tatiana, and Anastasia, descend from the train and climb into them. Finally the sick Tsarevich was lifted out and carried over to join them. As soon as they were all in, an order was given, and the horses moved off at a trot with their escort.

Gilliard, watching too, saw the Grand Duchesses burdened with valises and personal belongings; he noticed how Tatiana's feet sank into the treacherous, slimy mud as she carried her little dog and tried at the same time to drag a heavy brown case. When Nagorny attempted to help her, soldiers pushed him roughly aside. After another wait in the grey sheeting rain, they were shunted back to Ekaterinburg station, and Tatishchev, Countess Hendrikov, and Mlle Schneider were removed under guard – it appeared, to the town prison. Four servants, the chef and a footman among them, were taken to the Ipatiev House. Nagorny arrived again to carry away baggage and the children's beds, all identical; comfortable nickel-plated camp-beds modelled on one that Tsar Alexander II had used during the Turkish war.

Finally, to their great surprise, Rodionov came at five o'clock and said to those remaining – the tutors and some household servants – 'You are free and can go wherever you like.' Baroness Buxhoeveden was then transferred to their coach. Outside, the incessant rain poured down upon Ekaterinburg.

On the train to Ekaterinburg. Gilliard is on the left.

House of Special Purpose

The House of Special Purpose stood upon the highest of the low hills upon which Ekaterinburg (now Sverdlovsk),* town of miners and metal-workers, had been built on the east slope of the 'Red' Urals. Set upon a fairly steep incline on a corner site, this florid, two-storey house of stone set in a small garden belonged to a wealthy merchant, N. N. Ipatiev; in April he had received twenty-four hours' notice to leave. Before Nicholas and Alexandra arrived, men had put up a wooden fence very close to the wall, hiding house and garden and reaching to the windows of the upper floor. Later another fence hid the building completely up to the eaves and enclosed also the front entrance and gateway. The lower floor was made into guardrooms and offices; the upper one became a prison, the glass of its double windows whitewashed so that no one could look from them. Inside and out, the Bolsheviks established an intricate system of sentries and machine-gun posts.

On the arrival of the second party from Tobolsk, twelve people were packed into the five rooms. Nicholas, Alexandra, and Alexis shared one that faced a large square with the church of the Ascension. The Grand Duchesses had another, and Dr Botkin, the family's faithful physician, and four servants (maid, footman, chef, kitchen-boy), shared the rest. The men of the first garrison, brawling revolutionaries, were former factory workers of Ekaterinburg; three of them, armed with revolvers, kept constant watch outside the Imperial rooms. The commander of the inner guard, Avadeiev, was a loud-mouthed bully who enjoyed raging against the ex-Tsar as 'Nicholas the Blood-Drinker'. As a matter of course, all family requests were refused; guards entered the rooms when they felt like it, and even followed the girls to the lavatory which

* After Jacob Sverdlov, Chairman of the Central Executive Committee of the All-Russian Congress of Soviets.

they had scrawled over with obscene pictures of Alexandra and Rasputin.

The prisoners could be defiant. While, below them, the soldiers shouted their revolutionary songs, 'You Do Not Need a Golden Idol' or 'Get Cheerfully in Step, Comrades', Alexandra and her daughters would often join in such hymns as the Kheruvimskaya (Cherubim) Song to deaden the noise.

They could do nothing else but endure: brief afternoon exercise – little was permitted – reading, needlework: Alexis, confined to bed, had a ship model to amuse him and made small wire chains for it. Much later Gibbes was to find and photograph an undated letter which he believed was the last that the Tsarevich ever wrote. It was addressed to his old companion, Dr Derevenko's son Colia:

Dear Colia,

All sisters send greetings to you, mother, and grandmother. I feel well myself. How is grandmother's health? What is [illegible] doing? My head was aching all day, but now the pain has gone completely. I embrace you warmly . . . Greetings to Botkins from all of us.

Always yours,

ALEXIS

Cheerful enough; yet discipline was as harsh as it could be. Anastasia, unable to bear the claustrophobic effect of the white-washed windows, opened one and looked out. Immediately the

The Ipatiev house, Ekaterinburg, the 'House of Special Purpose' in which the Imperial Family was confined and murdered (from a faded photograph).

Alexis's last letter.

Drawing-room in the Ipatiev house.

sentry on duty fired his rifle, just missing her; the bullet lodged in the woodwork at her side.

It was at mealtimes that the prisoners most felt their position. Food could be scanty: black bread and tea for breakfast; at two o'clock, re-warmed soup and cutlets sent from a Soviet public dining-room, and placed in a single dish upon a table covered with greasy oilcloth: no linen or silver. Avadeiev would burst in now and then to grab a piece of meat from the pot. Alexandra could take nothing but macaroni; but she had always eaten very little indeed; Gibbes used to wonder how her frugal meals at Tobolsk kept her alive. Later, when the family could have food prepared in its own kitchen, the quality improved.

One morning, not long after the arrival, Nagorny, the endeared sailor-servant, was taken away. He had insisted, against the soldiers' committee, that Alexis needed two pairs of boots: a pair in reserve

The dining-room where the Imperial Family ate their last meal.

if the first were wet. Hard upon this a soldier had seized a gold chain, hanging from the bed, on which the boy had strung his collection of holy images. High in anger, Nagorny stopped the theft and was instantly arrested. Gibbes, still in Ekaterinburg, happened that day to be walking on the Vesnesensky Prospect, close to the Ipatiev house, with Gilliard and Dr Derevenko. Suddenly they saw Nagorny entering a carriage with Red Guards, their bayonets fixed. Simultaneously he saw his friends; without making a single betraying gesture he was driven off to Ekaterinburg prison, and there, after sharing a cell for four days with the first Prime Minister of the Provisional Government, Prince Lvov, he was taken out and shot.

In future Nicholas had himself to carry Alexis – now ill all the time – for the day's brief wheel-chair exercise in a dusty garden. The ex-Tsar's beard was getting grey. He wore a soldier's khaki

Nagorny.

The Grand Duchesses' bedroom. An enamel chamber-pot still stands in the corner of the room.

shirt with an officer's belt buckled round his waist; trousers and old, worn boots; on his breast his cross of St George. Alexandra (said one of the guards) 'had the appearance and manner of a grave, haughty woman'; but some of the fanatical soldiers were impressed, against their will, by Nicholas's simplicity, his kind eyes, and the feeling – expressed later in Maurice Baring's sonnet, 'Epitaph' – that

> Bereft of crown, and throne, and hearth, and name,
> Grief lent him majesty, and suffering
> Gave him a more than regal diadem.

Towards the middle of June, in this hot and dragging summer, there were the usual cloudy hopes of a rescue attempt. They stayed cloudy; the anxious monarchists never found a workable plan. Now the end was coming indeed. Avadeiev and his guards, so it was rumoured, had been growing too lenient; they were replaced by men of the Secret Police, five of them Magyars. The commander, Jacob Yurovsky, was a cold, sinister chief executioner. He had been given the order to kill because Bolshevism at that moment was engaged on several fronts. Even a Czech Legion (that had grown in the last year or so to some 60,000 men) was fighting its way through Siberia. Ekaterinburg might fall to the

'Whites' within a few days, so the Imperial Family must be swiftly obliterated. The place for the murder, a semi-basement room in the House of Special Purpose; thereafter, destruction of the bodies at an abandoned iron-mineshaft, a dozen miles off, a site known as the tract of the 'Four Brothers' because, according to legend, four pine trees used to grow from a pair of old stumps close to the road.

Twice a priest named Father Storozhev had been to the Ipatiev house to conduct a service. On 19 May/2 June he thought that Alexandra showed signs of fatigue but that Nicholas was calm and the Grand Duchesses were almost happy. The Tsarevich lay on a folding cot: 'I was shocked by his appearance [Storozhev said some months later]. He was gaunt and so very tall I was astounded. In general, his appearance was of one extremely sick. Only his eyes were alive and bright, looking at me, a new person, with noticeable interest. He had on a white shirt and was covered to the waist with a blanket.' On 1/14 July, nearly six weeks later, Storozhev was called again to celebrate Mass. This time he felt strongly that, though Alexis, in a wheel-chair, looked healthier, Nicholas and his daughters were exhausted. The deacon, as he walked back with the priest, said: 'Something has happened to them there. They seem to be some other people.' (One day the phrase would be snatched at by supporters of a perverse theory that the Imperial Family left Ekaterinburg unharmed.)

The last entry in Nicholas's published journal is on 30 June/13 July. Here it is, with others from the same week (though the diary has never been authenticated and is believed by some critics to be a Soviet fabrication):

25 June/8 July, Monday: Our life has not changed a bit under Yu[rovsky]. He comes into the bedroom to make sure that the seal on the box is unbroken [a box containing the family's gold objects, rings, bracelets, etc.] and looks out of the open window. All morning today, and up until four o'clock, they were testing and fixing the electric lights. Inside the house there are new guards, Letts, but outside they are the same—part soldier, part worker! According to rumour, several of Avadeiev's guards have already been arrested!

The door to the shed containing our baggage has been sealed. If only that had been done a month ago!

28 June/11 July, Thursday: About 10.30 in the morning three workers came to the open window, raised a heavy grating, and fastened it from the outside—without any warning from Yu[rovsky]. We like this type less and less.

Inside the 'House of Special Purpose'. The Empress's wheelchair is in the shadow on the right.

III

The room in which they were shot.

I began to read Volume VIII of Saltikov.

30 June/13 July, Saturday: Alexis took his first bath since Tobolsk. His knee is getting better, but he cannot straighten it out completely. The weather is warm and pleasant. We have no news whatever from outside.

On the morning of 3/16 July Yurovsky made his final dispositions; under his command the House of Special Purpose had become in effect a branch of the Cheka (the 'Extraordinary Commission for Combating Counter-Revolution and Speculation' or secret police). The young kitchen-boy was sent away from the house. In the afternoon Nicholas and his daughters walked normally in the garden. In the evening Yurovsky assembled his picked guards; the whole Imperial Family, he said, was to be shot. Just after midnight he went up to awaken his prisoners, telling them that there were urgent reasons why they must be moved. Inured to such alarms as these, they washed, dressed, and put on their outdoor clothes ready for another journey into the unknown. Alexandra wore her overcoat. Some carried pillows into which jewels had been stitched. Alexis, very sleepy, was in his father's arms. Anastasia was carrying her tiny dog.

Yurovsky led them downstairs into the yard, through a separate doorway to the lower floor, and at length to a vaulted, unfurnished semi-basement room, sixteen feet by eighteen, with a double window heavily grated. They would wait here for a while; at Nicholas's request Yurovsky sent for chairs. When they came Alexandra sat in one by the window and Nicholas took a second, supporting Alexis on his arm and shoulder as the boy rested across the third chair. Behind them, almost as if a group photograph were being taken, were the Grand Duchesses, Dr Botkin, and cook, valet and maid, the very tall Anna Stepanovna Demidova. One of the pillows she had brought she put now behind Alexandra's back; the other she held tightly.

A fleeting pause; then the Cheka guard tramped in, all with heavy revolvers. Yurovsky stepped forward; it is not known precisely what he said; the last phrase seems to have been: 'We are compelled to shoot you.' Nicholas half rose, still holding Alexis. He had begun to speak when Yurovsky shot him in the head and he died at once. Alexandra made the sign of the Cross before she, too, was killed. All fell except Demidova; the killers seized rifles from the next room and bayoneted her more than thirty times as she ran screaming by the wall with only a pillow to protect her. Just for a moment Alexis, moaning, moved his hand and Yurovsky fired at him again, twice or three times. Anastasia had merely fainted; coming to suddenly, she screamed, whereupon she was at once bayoneted and beaten to death. A guard smashed her dog's head with the butt of a rifle.

Rolled up in sheets and covered with mats, the corpses were packed into a lorry which reached the Four Brothers by dawn. There in the woods encircled by a cordon of Red Guards, the grim process of hacking, sawing, and burning in a petrol-fed bonfire – with sulphuric acid used for the larger bones – continued for fully three days.* What remained was hurled down the mine-shaft. More than a week afterwards a White army took Ekaterinburg. It found the Ipatiev house empty; the semi-basement room, scrubbed though it had been with sand, sawdust, and water, bore blood smears and stains, with the scars of many bullets and bayonet-thrusts; plaster had fallen from the walls.† In the court-yard, half starved, was the sole survivor of the Imperial Family, the Tsarevich's spaniel which one of the guards had stolen. Its name was Joy.

Jacob Yurovsky, the man who murdered the Imperial Family.

Joy.

---

* Ekaterinburg, said Robert Wilton, being the centre of the platinum industry, needed large stocks of sulphuric acid to generate the intense heat necessary for melting this hardest of metals. 'I wanted to order a platinum ring at a local jeweller's during my stay in the city 1919.' He could not carry out the order because there was no sulphuric acid 'since the previous year'.

† Robert Wilton (Special Correspondent of *The Times*), *The Last Days of the Romanovs* (London, 1920), with depositions of Pavel Medvedev and Anatoly Yakimov, guards at the Ipatiev house. Nicolas Sokolov, *Enquête judiciaire sur l'assassinat de la famille impériale russe* (Paris, 1924). Sokolov was the lawyer who investigated the murder.

Survivors

After the morning of 11/24 May on which Gibbes, Baroness Buxhoeveden and others of the suite and servants saw the three Grand Duchesses and the Tsarevich for the last time, they remained in Ekaterinburg for about ten days, using their own fourth-class rail-wagon as a base. Rodionov, who had told them at first that they were free, soon modified this. Instead, they were to return to the place they had come from, Tobolsk; but they could not obey because the advancing White army cut off the route. The rail system was utterly muddled. Until mid-June they had to occupy themselves in Ekaterinburg, feverish for news of the Imperial Family that no one could give them. Their one glimpse of Nagorny had suggested much. Again and again Gibbes walked by the Ipatiev house, masked by its double palisade and fiercely guarded; he saw nothing but a woman's hand opening an upper window and guessed that it might have been Alexandra's maid Anna Stepanovna Demidova.

Eventually their wagon – eighteen persons in it – was attached to a train that, with any luck, should have reached Tyumen on the following day. It was no hour for luck; they did not get far. At Kamyshlov the train was halted for ten days in a dirty little town, heavy with disease. Protest did nothing.

Still, as Gibbes wrote to his Aunt Kate a few months afterwards, 'We managed to get our wagon unhooked and attached to a train that was going on farther, and so in the course of a few hours we arrived at the station [Tyumen] where we had to leave the railway to take the boat for Tobolsk.'

By then, as he said elsewhere, the civil war was moving like a wall of fire across Siberia.

Tobolsk [he told Aunt Kate], which was another day and a half farther on, had passed out of the hands of the late [Red] Government

Gibbes's railway ticket from Ekaterinburg to Tyumen.

and was in the hands of a new [White] one. So the late Government refused us its permission and we had to stop at Tyumen. For a couple of weeks we all lived in the railway carriage at the station until we got accommodation. I found a very nice room at the top of a nice house overlooking the town; there were five windows and I could see all round. Not much furniture in the room, just necessaries; not even there, you would think, for there was no washstand. I had a bed, three chairs, and two tables. At first I used to go down to the kitchen, get a basin, and take it down to the wash-house and wash there till the horrid landlady objected, and then I had to manage in my bedroom: not so nice for it was impossible to spill much water.

Eventually, in mid-August, after Ekaterinburg had been taken by the Whites, he was able to return and settle there for a while, not knowing what his future might be. He continued to write, in snatches, a letter to Aunt Kate which was not posted for some weeks.

Passport issued to Gibbes on 31 July/ 13 August 1918 at Tobolsk. He is described rather inaccurately as a teacher, aged 37, 5 ft 10 ins tall, with light brown hair, high forehead, small nose, average mouth, and rounded chin. His place of birth is given as Rotterdam instead of Rotherham.

Countess Hendrikov.

I came here [10 Soldatskaya Street, Ekaterinburg] six weeks ago. For the last month I have been giving lessons and am already very busy, working four days a week and resting three as I feel somewhat tired still. This is a very quiet place, though it is a fairly large town. Nothing hardly has happened since I came, but I have seen a few English people. There are several resident in the town besides which we had the Commissioner, Sir Charles Eliot . . . He didn't stay long and lived all the time in his railway carriage at the railway station. Lately we have had military people. I was at the Consulate to dinner on Tuesday and it was crowded with them; many of them I had seen either in Petrograd or at the Stavka in 1916.

I have so often thought about you and wondered how you are. I couldn't send any news, anyhow. At the present time we are cut off from Petrograd and I have to send this through Vladivostok, right round the world. I suppose you will get it in about two months, but never mind, it may still be 'news', for I don't suppose I shall be able to send any by any other route.

He added a postscript:

It is a bright, sunny morning, or it will be when the sun is up . . . At this present moment it is freezing. I am not looking forward to a journey to Tyumen that I must make at the end of next week. When I came here two months ago I did not bring my luggage with me as I was not quite sure what I should do and it seemed useless to drag it about. Since then it has become more and more difficult, but now I must go or freeze for I have no winter clothes here. In summer when we came it was not such a serious matter, and it will be worse later when it becomes really cold. At present it is only the nights that are really cold. There are no 'class' carriages on the railway, only goods trucks, covered in but not heated. However, it is not a long journey, so that it will not matter much. For some time it was difficult to accommodate oneself to the new conditions of life, but now one is about used to everything. There is practically no sugar here. It can be got, but it costs about thirty roubles a pound, or what should be three pounds sterling, so naturally I take my tea without. Just recently I had some saccharine given to me and received it with great joy, but when I put some in my tea I found I didn't like it sweet, so I look at the saccharine and give it to visitors.

At the beginning of his letter, posted on 31 October [N.S.], Gibbes had said in a resolute understatement: 'We have not had a very gay time, and what has become of all the family we do not yet know for sure. Although there is some chance that all may be well, I begin to fear the worst.' He had already been given permission to visit the Ipatiev house; in the semi-cellar he was deeply shocked by the bullet-holes – particularly in the floor – and by traces of what had been a pool of the victims' blood. Gilliard, less affected, still believed when he left that the family might be alive. It was the faintest of hopes, though in time romantics would construct their own myth. As yet there had been no independent investigation; but an official Soviet statement in the newspaper *Izvestia* for 19 July [N.S.] had said simply and with one glaring falsehood (on which many monarchists, as well as Gilliard and Gibbes, based a faint hope):

Lately the approach of the Czecho-Slovak bands seriously threatened the capital of the Red Urals, Ekaterinburg. At the same time a new plot of counter-revolutionists which had, as its objective, the taking of the royal hangman out of the hands of the Soviet Government, was disclosed. In view of this the presidium of the Ural Territorial Soviet decided to shoot Nicholas Romanov which was done on July 16. The wife and son of Nicholas Romanov were sent to a safe place. The All-Russian Soviet Executive Committee, through its presidium, recognises as correct the decisions of the Ural Territorial Soviet.

Workers of Ekaterinburg had assembled in their town theatre on the night before any announcement appeared in their local paper, which printed it three days after *Izvestia*. Receiving the news with a generally triumphant cheer (though, even so, one or two men were faint-hearted enough to cry 'Show us the body!') they agreed that 'the execution of Nicholas the Bloody serves as an answer and threatening warning to the bourgeois-monarchist counter-revolution which attempts to drown in blood the workers' and peasants' revolt.'

The workers and peasants had been doing ably themselves. On the night after the death of the Imperial Family, six other Romanovs, a Grand Duke, a Grand Duchess (Elizabeth, the ex-Empress's devout sister), and four Princes were murdered in the northern Urals. The Grand Duke Michael had already been shot in the woods near Perm. Just outside Perm during early September – while Gibbes was working in Ekaterinburg – Countess Hendrikov and Mlle Schneider were executed. Prince Dolgoruky and Count Tatishchev simply vanished.

Mlle Schneider.

Diplomatic Secretary

Gibbes was in Ekaterinburg through the winter of 1918. On 23 December/5 January 1919, he wrote, still from 10 Soldatskaya Street, to Claudia Mikhailovna Bitner, a teacher with whom in the autumn of 1917 he had travelled on the river steamer from Tyumen up to Tobolsk. She was in Tobolsk when he wrote:

Please accept my very best wishes for Christmas and the New Year. I hope you may get this before the latter but there is no chance of it arriving for the former. You will know I am thinking of all in Tobolsk and the great change that a single year has made to us all. Indeed it is a very sad Christmas this year and I shall be very glad when it is over.

When I was in Tyumen a month ago I received a letter from you and posted I do not know how many weeks previously. It had been disinfected, and by the time I received it, it was already several weeks old. I did not even know that it was there, or I would have written sooner, for you must have thought me very remiss in not answering it before. I was very pleased to get it, for I had been thinking that you had forgotten my humble existence.

Perm is taken! [in the Northern Urals; taken by the Whites]. Agreeable to my promise when I was in Tobolsk, I went at once to the telegraph office to try and send a telegram to your mother, but they told me it will be a long time before they are able to send messages as the lines are all down. I therefore searched among my acquaintance to find someone going to Perm who promised to take charge of a letter, carry it to Perm, and post it there. I wrote a few lines saying that you are well (as I hope is indeed the case) and that you are living at Tobolsk at the same address . . .

There is no good news to send, and as far as I have heard, the taking of Perm has not yet thrown more light on what took place here in July. I am told that there is little real doubt as to the fate of those we love, but at the same time it is not yet proved. I heard that several Commissars had been taken at Perm but no one here knows yet what has happened. The Judicial authorities have been gone more

The railway station at Perm (now Molotov).

than a week, but travelling is so slow (and they work so badly) that there has been hardly any time to receive any details, but in the main I fear that no news is bad news.

I have received a letter from Gilliard in which he tells me that the Colonel [Kobylinsky] has just been to Tyumen and has been appointed Commander of the Garrison. Please give him my heartiest good wishes on his appointment.

Do you remember the very beautiful crucifix you got Denesov to carve for me? Might I ask you to get him to do me another? I should also like the kind of comb he made for Anna Stepanovna [Demidova]. He makes very nice combs and the other man's were very bad. I shall be so grateful. I am teaching English to the unenlightened of Ekaterinburg and get along comfortably enough. The town is better than Tyumen but dull enough for all that and very cold, worse in that respect than Tobolsk for here there is always a wind (generally from the north).

He would soon be away from the unenlightened of Ekaterinburg. Writing to Aunt Kate in October, he had told her that Sir Charles Eliot, British High Commissioner for Siberia, who had

Admiral Kolchak.

been in the town, had promised to send home a telegram for him. By then the military map was turbulently animated. Soon after the German-Soviet treaty at Brest-Litovsk (which the Russians would denounce eight months later) the Allies, by way of Murmansk and Archangel, had begun to make dispositions in the north. There was a more ambitious landing at Archangel early in August; previously, other troops – including many Japanese – had entered by Vladivostok in the Far East. Added to these were forces from Europe including a Czech Legion, of some 60,000 men, composed of a brigade that had been formed in Russia in 1914, augmented now by many Czech and Slovak prisoners-of-war and deserters. During the spring the Czechs had been moving up towards Vladivostok in groups in order to be transported thence to the Western Front in Flanders. The Bolsheviks, prompted by the Germans, decided to disarm them whereupon the Czechs, reacting violently, managed within a short time to command a large section of the Trans-Siberian railway and to sweep in as what was described hopefully as 'the vanguard of the Allied forces'. A White Russian provisional government was set up at Omsk, and in mid-November Admiral Alexander Vaslevich Kolchak, then forty-five years old, became Supreme Regent after a *coup d'état*. A difficult, repressive man, he would soon be on the worst of terms with the Czechs; but for the moment the Whites continued to advance. At the time of his letter to Gibbes Sir Charles Eliot was accredited to Kolchak at Omsk as British High Commissioner for Siberia. A popular Siberian song contained the phrase: 'Uniform, British; boot, French; bayonet, Japanese; ruler, Omsk.'

Undoubtedly Gibbes's record and his knowledge of Russian must have pleased Sir Charles. On 10/23 January 1919, a letter reached Soldatskaya Street from Thomas Preston, Ekaterinburg's steadfast British Consul. The High Commissioner, he said, offered Gibbes a post 'as a secretary on his staff at Omsk, on the terms mentioned in his telegram of 20 January, viz. £25 sterling monthly, with board and lodging. Sir Charles, in his telegram of 22 January, states that a compartment on his train will be placed at your disposal. If you are agreeable to accept these terms, His Excellency wishes you to leave with the utmost despatch.'

Gratefully, he did so. In a letter to a cousin that spring, sending some photographs for possible sale, he said: 'I trust you will do all you can to help me to retrieve my fallen fortunes.

As you can well believe, I have lost heavily in all these troubles.' Omsk, where Sir Charles expected to stay, was transiently the anti-Bolshevik centre, the capital of White Russia, and described then, important though it was, as 'very much of an overgrown steppe village'. Gibbes for a while was not stationed there, at first he went out to the Far East, to Vladivostok. Before this, at Ekaterinburg on 13/26 January, a Sunday, he noted in his brief diary: 'Finished everything. Left cards on the Commandant and his lady . . . I have been very surprised at the warmth of people's feelings. I had no idea I was so appreciated.' A month later, in Vladivostok, the days were more monotonous than he had hoped: a steady round of translation and cyphering. On 25 February [N.S.] he wrote in his diary: 'I feel awfully depressed; don't like this life much; in fact, I'm awfully tired.' Various entries begin: 'Translation all day' or 'Worked at translation all day.' But there is a longer note on 28 February:

General Dieterichs.

Called on General [Michael] Dieterichs [one of Admiral Kolchak's principal aides] in his train at the railway station as he requested me through the High Commissioner today. While I was there the Commander of H.M.S. *Kent* came to ask about the things he was to receive from General Dieterichs. The General said that the things as yet were all in boxes and he had ordered cases to be made (20 cases, 1 metre long by $\frac{3}{4}$ high and wide), but they were not yet ready. The Commander said that the goods were to be transferred to the Bank of England for custody. General Dieterichs said that he had over 1000 articles that had belonged to the Imperial Family, including the chairs (the long chair used by the Empress and the chair on wheels from the Ipatiev house), and poor Joy [the dog] . . . He showed me many photographs of the things including the diamonds (two) and pearl earring and small Maltese cross with emeralds. The most terrible was the photograph of the finger showing it was clean cut off. He said that expert evidence was unanimous in declaring that the finger had belonged to a woman of over 35 years who had been accustomed to manicure her hands. They were not sure which finger it was, but thought that it was the first finger, though . . . it might have been the third. He also showed me a book containing verses beginning I pray' in the handwriting of the Empress and addressed to [the Grand Duchess Olga] – probably Christmas 1917, being similar to my card.*
He also asked me about Alexis and said that from entries in the diary it would seem that he was quite a child, and I said that owing to his illness it was so, but that in some respects he was older than his years.

* Reproduced on page 87.

Kolchak's headquarters at Omsk.

When he had any diplomatic business with regard to Court arrangements he always showed great tact and judgment. We spoke of the Countess Hendrikov and her diary which has fallen in its entirety into the hands of the government . . .

In Sir Charles Eliot's train on 5 June [N.S.], Gibbes, bound west for Omsk, was writing to Aunt Kate, copying his letter on paper headed 'University of Hong Kong' of which Eliot had been Vice-Chancellor.

We have been travelling just a week [he wrote]. First, let me say that my address remains the same as before: 'The British High Commission, Vladivostok, via America.' All letters will be forwarded, wherever we may be . . .

I must tell you about the train: a very fine collection of railway carriages. The High Commissioner has a coach almost to himself, and has a study, bedroom, and bathroom; while there is another compartment for his private secretary. On one side of him there is the dining-car, divided into two compartments, one of which has a long dining-table with seats for eight or ten which can be extended to seat another four, and the other has seats and chairs and tables and serves as a sort of sitting-room for everybody. On the other side of him there is a first-

class coach containing a number of separate compartments. One double compartment has been turned into an office or Chancery as it is more correctly called, and contains a safe, stationery cabinet, a couple of tables, and a typewriter, instead of the usual seats which have been removed. I have also a similar compartment and a writing table which can also serve as an office on occasion. Then there are other compartments of the usual kind, all full, for we are a more numerous company than was at first expected, being in all seven officials and four soldiers.

Presently he gets his first impression of a town that later he would know and love, Harbin, on the southern bank of the Sungari river, and the centre of Tsarist activities in Manchuria in the generation after the October rising:

We left Vladivostok on Thursday evening, 29 May, and travelled straight to Harbin which we reached on Saturday morning. It was a very beautiful day and I had some shopping to do in the morning in what is called the new town. We then had lunch in the train, and afterwards I went down with the Railway Transport Officer on an engine to the place where he was getting our supply of kerosene which we need for the electric light plant. When we got there, outside the town, I got off and went away on my own to the mixed Russian-Chinese town on the bank of the river and wandered about all the afternoon among the Chinese and enjoyed it very much.

They seem to swarm everywhere, like ants more than human beings, but they are so merry and bright, so smiling and cheerful, so knowing and inquisitive, crowding round you if you ever stop. In their manners they are most unconventional, doing everything in public which most people do in private. I had still a few things to buy and went into a shop where I was immediately beset by all the shop boys, a great number of them with apparently nothing whatever to do . . . I thoroughly enjoyed my first view of the Far East and its wonderful life. As the sun got low, people stopped work and began their evening meal in the street, eating a mess of pottage of different kinds, one a sort of macaroni made of rice, while another was a kind of thin gruel; all, of course, drank tea in bowls without any handles.

When their inner needs were satisfied, they often had a gamble with one of the professional gamblers who abound there. The game they play I could hardly discover, but it consists in the use of a number of dominoes with the figures in black or red . . . In the end I had to hurry back to the station as I was afraid to miss the train which was due to pull out at ten o'clock . . .

They came to Chita where the train paused a few hours, long enough for Gibbes to go out to the market; he bought a zinc foot-bath for use in the train, an old brass candlestick for his coupé when the electric light ran out, and an earthenware jar for the flowers he had just gathered. 'The night before our arrival I had an interesting conversation with a young officer to whom we gave a lift. He was an ardent monarchist and wore the Romanov ribbon with a small embossed Imperial crown on it, on his left breast. He declined to tell me the whole of its significance, but he had an undying faith in the family that was most touching.' (It was a faith Gibbes shared.)

Then:

After Chita the train runs through very beautiful country, and the main cause of my having abandoned this letter (I am now writing in Omsk) was that it seemed a shame not to look out of the window. As you go further on, the train approaches the great Baikal Lake, and for the greater part of the day we were running along its shore. Often the track runs just above the water, and the eastern part was most picturesque as there were still large blocks of ice floating on the water which in the sunlight became a delicate green . . .

[On to Irkutsk.] We were told that the train would arrive about

The British High Commissioner's train.

nine o'clock at Irkutsk. Having given this information, the station-master or the engine-driver or somebody proceeded to astonish us. The train began to move at what you may describe as 'a hell of a lick'. Things were thrown about; my typewriter rolled off its stool, and our safe which it takes several people to lift, travelled across the room all by itself.

We had not counted on getting in so soon. The British Consul was in the stationmaster's office asking when we should arrive, and being told at eleven, when the train steamed in. Unfortunately the Consul brought several telegrams which had to be de-cyphered and their answers to be cyphered; tedious work which took two hours and prevented us going outside the train. The stationmaster, who wanted to get rid of us, said it would be safest and best to leave as quickly as possible, and we steamed out at eleven without my ever going outside the station. This is the second time I have gone through Irkutsk without seeing anything of the city, which is the finest in Siberia.

The next morning we were well on our way into the danger zone . . .

The letter ends there; but nothing could have happened in the danger zone, for Gibbes was in Omsk, enjoying the freedom of its diplomatic life. He had plenty of friends. Even as early as January he had got from an Ekaterinburg friend a letter to a Staff-Captain Zubov at the H.Q., Supreme Command, Political Section: 'I take the liberty of addressing Comrade Gibbes to you; he will perhaps be in need of your assistance. You will find him not only interesting but perhaps even very helpful company.'

The Four Brothers

Not much more than a year after he had watched Nagorny bearing the Tsarevich away through the rain for the last time, Gibbes – who would never have thought of himself as 'Comrade' – had gone from Omsk to Ekaterinburg to help Nicolas Sokolov, a lawyer with the title of Investigating Magistrate for Cases of Special Importance of the Omsk Tribunal. Both Gibbes and Gilliard (who would remain three years in Siberia before returning to Switzerland) acted as advisers.* So did some of their former colleagues in the Imperial household.

There had already been a superficial inquiry into the night at the house of Ipatiev and those ensuing days by the Ganina mine on the tract of the 'Four Brothers'. But the task did need someone of Sokolov's acuteness and obsessive persistence. In the spring of 1919 General Dieterichs, acting for the 'Supreme Regent', Admiral Kolchak, had shown to him all relics that had been recovered from the house itself and elsewhere in Ekaterinburg, and from the debris at the place of cremation. Gibbes and Gilliard, as soon as they had returned to the house from Tyumen in the previous August, had seen the charred objects that filled the stoves in the House of Special Purpose: portrait frames, brushes of various kinds, a jewel-case covered in lilac silk and lined with white satin, a little basket in which the Tsarevich used to keep his hairbrushes. A great deal else was found in the stoves, the rubbish bins, round the house, and in the illicit possession of former guards. There were numerous icons and several books, many of them owned by Tatiana: one, *Les Bienfaits de la Vierge,* inscribed in Alexandra's hand, half in English, half in Russian: 'For my darling Tatiana fr. her loving old Mama. Tobolsk,

* Gilliard was married to Alexandra Tegleva, who had been nurse to the Grand Duchesses and the Tsarevich, and who shared the imprisonment at Tsarskoe Selo and Tobolsk. She proceeded to Ekaterinburg, but was one of those turned back to Tyumen.

January 12, 1918.' The Tsarevich had owned a book on how to play the balalaika and a diary for 1916 with notes by Gibbes and Gilliard on his occupations and his health. His journal, stolen by one of the guards and written entirely in the boy's hand, began on 11/24 March 1917 and ended on 9 November with the words: 'Today has passed like yesterday and also sadly.'

Still, nothing was so dramatic as the evidence that accumulated by the mine at the 'Four Brothers', a clay-surface tract – clay thrown up when the mine was being worked – in the woods a few miles from Lake Isetsk; furrowed soil, one open shaft, water brimming in the disused workings. Here, with Sokolov, Robert Wilton (of *The Times*), and others, Gibbes stood on a summer day in his cloth cap and belted overcoat, imagining what had happened in the bleakness lit by the flare of those funeral pyres.

Objects belonging to the Imperial Family found by General Dieterichs (from a faded photograph). Those encircled are now in the Gibbes collection.

*Investigations at the mine at the
'Four Brothers'.*

The mine had long been abandoned. After the murders, and the Bolsheviks' retreat from Ekaterinburg, there were immediate discoveries. Peasants of a tiny village, Koptyaki, seeking to know what Red soldiers had been doing in the birch woods and why no one was permitted to enter, had found, close to a shaft, the remnants of a large bonfire. Such things were scattered about as corset whalebones, braces buckles, slippers, dress fasteners, and a cross with green stones (the ex-Empress's emerald pectoral cross). Later, officials who went to the spot unearthed a valuable diamond; Gilliard, testifying at a first inquiry, believed that this had been concealed in a button worn by either of the Grand Duchesses Olga or Tatiana.

After several months, a difficult gap, it took the deductive and scientific skills of Sokolov to reconstruct, beyond reasonable doubt, the posthumous fate of the Imperial Family of Russia. To this obscure loneliness the bodies had been borne through the dark; there, upon the clay area by the mine, they had been stripped, ruthlessly dissected, consumed by bonfires – one by the shaft, one near a birch tree – and then dissolved with sulphuric acid. Cinders

Sheets laid out to receive the human remains at the 'Four Brothers'.

and objects that remained unburned were thrown into the mine. Ice at the foot of the shaft had been smashed; when everything had sunk to the bottom of the water a false floor was let down and anchored. It was directly under the floor that Sokolov's searchers found the corpse of a small dog preserved by the ice, its right front paw broken and a hole in its skull. Gibbes recognised it; and on 27 June Sokolov placed this statement in the files:

Sydney Ivanovich Gibbes, aged 40 [he was 43], a British subject, at present secretary to the English diplomatic mission, testified:

Anastasia Nicolaievna had a small dog, some kind of Japanese breed, very small, with long hair; its colouring was black and ginger; the black hair on the upper parts of the body, the reddish hair on the lower parts. Its tail was long and long-haired; also its ears were long. It had several distinctive features. It had large, round eyes; its teeth were bared and were always visible; its tongue was very long and used to hang out of its mouth, I can't remember on which side. Its name was Gemmy;* it was so small that it was often carried. The whole family loved it, especially the Tsar.

* Or Jamie.

129

I maintain that the dog I saw today in the shaft was Gemmy. I noticed its hair, the shape of its eye sockets, and its teeth. It was undoubtedly the same.

When material from the two searches, especially from Sokolov's tireless sifting, had been put together, the testimony was plain. Thus (among much more) a buckle that had been exposed to intense heat was probably from the ex-Tsar's belt, and another – also of brass, with the Imperial crest – undoubtedly from the belt of the Tsarevich. Shoe buckles had belonged to one of the Grand Duchesses; an earring of platinum, pearl, and gold was Alexandra's (Gibbes: 'These were her favourite earrings and she wore them often'); a jubilee badge of a Lancer regiment, with sapphires and diamonds, she had worn on her bracelet; pieces of fabric, burned, torn, or cut, came from her clothing and the Grand Duchesses', from the Tsarevich's overcoat and his knapsack. A pocket case owned by Nicholas had held his wife's portrait. Six women were among the victims in the Ipatiev house; here now were six pairs of corset steels, as well as side bones, clasps, fasteners and hooks, and hooks for laces. Alexandra would not permit her daughters or her servants to go without corsets, and she invariably wore them herself.

Many jewels lay upon Sokolov's tarpaulins in a mass of shining fragments:* emeralds, rubies, sapphires, diamonds, pearls, topazes, almandines. When Alexandra, from Ekaterinburg, sent a code message back to Tobolsk, the women of the household had set to work to hide the Romanov jewels; and Alexandra Tegleva, the children's former nurse, explained to Sokolov how it was done. They put the jewels in wadding, covered it with two brassières of heavy linen, and then sewed these together and covered them with wadding on both sides. The Empress's jewels were hidden in two pairs of double brassières, each weighing four-and-a-half pounds in all and each containing brilliants, emeralds, and amethysts. The Grand Duchess Tatiana wore one and the Grand Duchess Anastasia the other:

The Grand Duchesses' jewels were sewn into a double brassière in the same way, and this (I don't know how much it weighed) was worn by Olga Nicolaievna. Besides, they carried many pearls on their bodies, under their blouses. We also sewed jewels into their hats,

---

* The fragments were later buried, it is said, in the Russian cemetery outside Paris.

between the lining and the velvet; I remember a large pearl necklace and a brooch with a large sapphire and brilliants.

The Grand Duchesses had blue outer garments of cheviot. These had sashes on each of which were two buttons; we ripped them off and in their place sewed jewels, brilliants I believe, wrapping them first in wadding and then in black silk. The Grand Duchesses had also grey garments of English tricot with black stripes: autumn clothing which they wore during the summer in bad weather. Here, as well, we ripped off the buttons and sewed on the jewels in black silk and wadding.

Investigators at the Four Brothers came upon bullets, a human finger from a middle-aged woman (long, slender, well-shaped, like Alexandra's hand), two pieces of human skin, and some pieces of human bone. A set of artificial teeth, discovered near the shaft, was identified as Dr Botkin's. When Sokolov did not know what to make of a mixed collection, bits of lead foil, four nails, a used revolver bullet, and two small copper coins, Gibbes recalled that Alexis had collected odds and ends and would go round in Tobolsk picking up old nails that 'one day' would be useful. So, in a sense, they were.

Fortifying scientific evidence was ample. Sokolov went on to question half-a-dozen witnesses at length. Colonel Kobylinsky, Gilliard, and Gibbes all described the life in exile. Three former Red Guards remembered the House of Special Purpose: the silence of the procession to the death-chamber ('During my presence', said one guard, Pavel Medvedev, 'none of the Tsar's family asked any questions; they did not weep or cry'); the screams of Demidova; the blood running across the floor; the mopping and scrubbing; then next day's silence: 'There was', said Anatoly Yakimov, 'nobody in the rooms; not a single sound was heard . . . Only their little dog [Joy] was standing near the door, waiting to be let into those rooms. I remember this so well because I thought: You are waiting in vain.'

Claimants

Many, the Dowager Empress Marie among them, waited in vain for the Tsar's return. To myriads of his subjects, whatever the Bolsheviks might decree, he had been a ruler by divine right, God's steward, deputy-elect: he could not have perished. Some simply refused to believe in a barbaric act, 'the nightmare picture,' General Dieterichs said, 'forced upon them by the rooms of the Ipatiev house'. A few decided it was all part of the vast deception called history; an arcane plot that must be exposed from time to time for the benefit of future generations whose own history would be exposed in its turn. From Ekaterinburg the inevitable clouds of rumour mounted; the family had escaped somehow, somewhere, a consummation devoutly to be wished. Theories have grown even more webbed with the years. They postulate an immense conspiracy. They say that it was all, in effect, a Bolshevik charade; that the Imperial Family had left Ekaterinburg, for some unknown destination, three weeks before the murder: an idea that involves, among much else, a prolonged game of catch-as-catch-can between Bolsheviks and Germans, the manipulation of Nicholas's journal, the planting of evidence (all those remains at the mine), and a variety of linked suppositions. It becomes as circumstantial as Sheridan's narrative of the bullet that 'struck a little bronze Shakespeare that stood over the fireplace, grazed out of the window at a right angle, and wounded the postman who was just coming to the door with a double letter from Northampton-shire.'

Once the stories begin they cannot be halted; further theories must be formed to cover other events. Though a year after Ekaterinburg the Bolsheviks admitted that the Imperial Family was dead and staged a 'trial' at Perm, indicting several 'Socialist revolutionaries of the left wing', the stories of survival continued to multiply. Where did the Imperial Family go? No one answered,* but numerous pretenders arrived – very soon, a mock-Tsarevich in Siberia, and, right down the years, several claimants to be the Grand Duchess Anastasia, last to be killed. It was relatively early when Gibbes, in April 1928, heard from a friendly journalist about 'a woman being taken very seriously in America as the daughter of the late Tsar, and even by some members of the Imperial Family'. Gibbes himself, in December 1928, wrote from St Stephen's House in Oxford, where he was taking a course, to the Grand Duke Alexander Mikhailovich in Paris:

I have the honour to acknowledge the receipt of your letter asking me to write my opinion on Mme Tchaikovsky's claim to be the Grand Duchess Anastasia.

In my opinion there is, unfortunately, no room for doubt that the Grand Duchess Anastasia perished at Ekaterinburg at the same time as the Emperor and Empress, the Tsarevich, and her three sisters, the Grand Duchess[es] Olga, Tatiana, and Marie, with Mlle Demidova and the rest. This fact, of itself, disposes of the claim now made by Mme Tchaikovsky. Additional facts of refutation are not wanting, but the essential point is found in the sad fact of the Grand Duchesses' death . . .

As soon as the way was open, after the retreat of the Bolshevik Government, I hastened to Ekaterinburg. Nothing beyond vague rumour, however, could be learned. It was not until the following summer, 1919, when a full investigation was made by Mr Sokolov, that the extent and horror of the tragedy was learnt. I visited the clearing in the forest outside Ekaterinburg and saw what had been recovered. Months of toil were involved in pumping out and washing the contents of the deep mine-shaft into which the remains from the bonfire had been thrown . . . All who actually took part in the investigation and inspected the remains were obliged to abandon hope that anyone had survived.

Only a few, of course, were able to form an opinion under these conditions which presented all the facts of the case. There were, however, plenty of interested persons who had nothing but rumour and garbled accounts to build upon. Among these the most extraordinary tales were circulated. Various Pretenders actually appeared while I was still in Siberia. Not being obsessed by any great faith in themselves, these people's courage quickly failed and they were easily confuted and exposed.

---

* A particularly good suggestion was quoted by Robert K. Massie (*Nicholas and Alexandra*) from Paul Bulygin. Here the entire Imperial Family was said to be in a ship cruising eternally through the White Sea without ever touching land.

The first legends concerning the Imperial children were in circulation as early as 1917 while we were still all living together in Tobolsk. At the end of that year the *Daily Graphic* printed a fantastic paragraph stating that the Grand Duchess Tatiana, one of the Tsar's daughters, had gone to America, etc., etc.; she was then actually sitting with me in a drawing-room at Tobolsk reading the news of herself. If such things happened in creditable newspapers in 1917, while they were still alive, what could not happen with credulous people after they were dead?

I have not had the advantage of seeing Mme Tchaikovsky in person but her photographs failed to invoke in me the slightest belief in her story, however much I wish that it were true. The evidence supplied by Mons. Bischoff is one of irrefutable force to anyone who has intimately known the Grand Duchess Anastasia Nicolaievna. There is one point, however, on which I can speak with paramount knowledge and authority. Mme Tchaikovsky has affirmed that I limp. Had I been dead, it might have been difficult to prove, but being yet alive and happily in full possession of both my legs, I am able to demonstrate that I limp only in the imagination of Mme Tchaikovsky.

I have the honour to remain Your Imperial Highness's humble servant.

The Anastasia stories lingered on. During the early 1950s the French dramatist Marcelle Maurette wrote a play on the subject (adapted by Guy Bolton and staged in London, 1953). History is prodigal in these legends. A French researcher, more than a quarter of a century ago, asked for possible confirmation of his belief that Joan of Arc had fled to England, and a *Times* leader-writer (in the days of the 'fourth leader') reflected sadly: 'Authentic news (for example) of the settling in Bermondsey, or Barking, about 1431, of a young woman with a strong French accent, a military gait, and a suspicious familiarity with French court gossip, is not the kind of thing that can be expected to reward inquirers at this distant time.' Anastasia is nearer; but that is all we can say.

Shortly after the murder, Leon Trotsky, who had been away from Moscow, met Sverdlov, Chairman of the Central Executive Committee (to whom Yakovlev had once telegraphed from Omsk). Where was the Tsar? Trotsky asked,[*] and received the reply: 'He has been shot . . . All of the family with him.'

'And who made the decision?'

'We decided it here,' Sverdlov said. 'Ilyich [Lenin] decided that we shouldn't leave the Whites a live banner to rally round . . .'

[*] Leon Trotsky, *Diary in Exile, 1935* (Harvard, 1953).

The Box

When Gibbes was with Sokolov on the tract of the Four Brothers in the summer of 1919 the Whites were retreating. Kolchak's offensive had been stopped at the end of April. In July the Red forces would take Perm; thence the retreat of Kolchak's troops became progressively disordered. On 14 July Ekaterinburg was recaptured, and by early August Kolchak had lost the entire industrial region of the Urals. It was only a matter of time before Omsk fell; on 15 November it did so. The British High Commision moved 1500 miles east to Irkutsk where Gibbes, in the previous June, as described in the letter to Aunt Kate, had stopped for only a couple of hours: the second occasion he had been through without seeing anything of the city, 'the finest in Siberia': 'From the distance it looks very much like all Russian towns built largely in the middle of last century, a number of churches with towers and cupolas and several large buildings of simple but harmonious proportions; many trees and gardens and the wooden houses of the rest of the town.' Now he had less than two months in Irkutsk before the High Commission, with Miles Lampson (later Lord Killearn) in place of Sir Charles Eliot, now Ambassador in Tokyo, was again evacuated. It moved to Verkhne Udinsk and, practically at once, out to the Far East. Behind, in that frozen winter, White resistance had almost dissolved: Kolchak, in Bolshevik hands, was summarily shot early in February 1920, and his body thrust under the ice of a tributary of the Angara river at Irkutsk. A month later the British High Commission in Siberia came quietly to an end.

Before Gibbes left he was involved for the last time in the story of the Imperial Family. The single-minded Sokolov, who had stayed at the tract of the Four Brothers until the twelfth hour – when indeed Red patrols were approaching the mine – had reached eastern Siberia with his boxes and dossiers. He was entirely persuaded that responsibility for the murder rested with both the Moscow Soviet and direct German pressure behind it. Now his persistent inquiries were endangering him in this confused country alive with cloak-and-dagger work and in the ebb of a failing war. But he had to preserve his material. During the British High Commission's halt at Verkhne Udinsk, the veteran White leader, General Michael Dieterichs, who had been with Sokolov at the mine and who had lately resigned his military post in profound disagreement with Kolchak, wrote to Miles Lampson:

7 January 1920

His Excellency the British High Commissioner.

To the last possible moment I wished to retain in my own hands and in Russia, in the revival of which I still continue to trust, the affair of the Imperial Family, i.e. the substantial evidence in the matter and the Remains of Their Imperial Majesties, which it has been possible to find on the place where Their Corpses were burnt.

The turn which events are taking, however, shows that in order to ensure the safety of these Sacred Relics, it is essential that They should not be connected with my fate.

I cannot leave Russia; the German orientation in Chita [further east in Siberia] may compel me temporarily to seek refuge in the forest. Under such conditions I am of course unable to carry with me the Great National Sacred Relics.

I have decided to entrust you, as the Representative of Great Britain, with the safe-keeping of these Sacred Objects. I think you will understand without my having to explain, why I wish it to be Great Britain: you and we have one common historical foe, and the tortuous murder of the Members of the Imperial Family, a deed unprecedented in history, is the deed of *this foe,* aided by their assistants, the Bolsheviks.

I should like to add that if circumstances compel you to take the Imperial Remains and the documents out of Russia, and if England cannot return them to me, I consider that they can be only handed over to the Grand Duke Nicholas Nicolaievich or General [A. L.] Denikin [commander of the Whites in S. Russia].

Allow me to wish you and your country every prosperity, firmly to withstand the storm raging in the whole world at present.

I take the liberty of respectfully wishing all prosperity and health to His Majesty, the King of England, and beg to remain,

Yours very sincerely,   M. DIETERICHS

A scribbled pencil note identifies the contents of the box:

This box, which once belonged to Her Majesty the Empress, now contains all that was recovered at the mine shaft from the remains of

The box in which the remains of the Imperial Family were placed, and which was for a while in Gibbes's charge.

the burned bodies of:

His Imperial Majesty Nicholas II, Her Imperial [space left here for the titles] and burned together with them: Doctor Eugene Sergeyevich Botkin, Servant Alexei Yegorovich Trupp, Cook Ivan Mikhailovich Kharitonov, and girl servant Anna Stepanovna Demidova.

5 January 1920
LT-GENERAL DIETERICHS

On 8 January Lampson received the box, entrusted – as he wrote in a later despatch to London – 'in dramatic circumstances at Verkhne Udinsk on the night of my departure from that station eastward'. He took it with him to Harbin. After some delay the American Consul-General reached the city with Sokolov and another, larger, box which was said to contain proof of German complicity in the murder. Both boxes were lodged for safe-keeping with the British Consul.

Gibbes, who went on with Lampson to Peking, wrote from there a memorandum to the Foreign Secretary (Lord Curzon), describing events at the mine near Ekaterinburg and Sokolov's present personal anxieties. The despatch had gone to London when Gibbes, 'my dear Sydney Ivanovich', got an urgent appeal from Sokolov in Harbin. The letter, from a man clearly under intense nervous strain, requested British safeguards for his boxes:

Skidelsky, the Harbin millionaire, a Jew, is a relative and near friend of Lev Bronstein (i.e. Trotsky): Bronstein is married to Skidelsky's sister. Mrs Skidelsky has recently visited Trotsky in

Moscow and brought from there a present . . . a ring with a light blue diamond which belonged to [the Grand Duchess] Tatiana Nicolaievna. She does not conceal this fact . . .

My dear Sydney Ivanovich, you must understand that I have far too much evidence not to be able to give you proof: that the real perpetrators of the Imperial affair are our common enemies, the Germans . . . At present I am surrounded by enemies: they are swarming all round me.

Sokolov was able to escape from his enemies to France. He continued with the task of which he said: 'The truth of the Tsar's death is the truth of the sufferings of Russia.' During three years at Fontainebleau, 1921–4, he wrote his detailed narrative, *Enquête judiciaire sur l'assassinat de la famille impériale russe*, published not long before he died on 23 November 1924. Towards the end there is a footnote:

At the moment of Admiral Kolchak's death I found myself in Harbin in a most difficult position. Wishing at all costs to save the dossiers of the inquiry, I wrote a letter in February 1920 to the English ambassador in Peking [the High Commissioner for Siberia], Mr Lampson, asking him if he could arrange to send the documents to Europe for me. I told him that these were the victims' remains and I emphasised the Germans' role in the affair. On 23 February the ambassador's secretary . . . told me that the ambassador had telegraphed to London for instructions. On 19 March the English government's reply was communicated to me by Mr Sley [Sly], the British Consul at Harbin. It was negative. On the same day I found the French General [Maurice] Janin,* who was in Harbin. Janin told General Dieterichs, who accompanied me, and myself, that he considered the mission we entrusted to him to be a debt of honour to a faithful ally. Thanks to him, the dossiers were saved and taken to a safe place.

What happened to the precious relics of the Imperial Family? Presumably this was the box that, according to Captain Paul Bulygin, Sokolov's assistant who shared his French apartment, had 'received the bones found among the ashes on the spot where the bones of the Imperial Family were burnt', and contained also thirteen carefully preserved drops of blood, as well as 'the Tsaritsa's finger . . . preserved in alcohol'. The box, still in existence in 1935, is said to be in the Janin family vault.

* Janin, chief of the French military mission, was commander of the Allied forces in Siberia. He said later that there were a strong-box and three heavy suitcases.

Customs Officer

When John Foster Fraser visited Harbin (now Pinkiang) some twenty years earlier, it was already an important and growing rail junction, and 'a magnet for all the adventurers in Russia'.

In Gibbes's day Harbin was the centre of Tsarist activity in Manchuria; it would remain so during the generation after the October rising of 1917. Gibbes had been strongly attracted to it and to its people. As he had written to Aunt Kate in June 1919:

> I enjoyed it very much . . . I tried to take some photographs, but the people are very shy of the camera and run away whenever they observe that they come within its range. They imagine that it affects their insides; while I was talking to one Chinese who was holding a baby, he kept on telling it not to be afraid when, as a matter of fact, the child never took any notice of the camera at all. It was a pretty scene as it grew dusk and the lights began to show here and there, with the hum of conversation and the ripple of laughter coming from the many groups: the streets are all narrow and full of people and seem to teem with life in the same way as does a hive of bees or an anthill, people appearing to walk round and over each other.

After the end of the High Commission in Siberia, he served briefly as a secretary at the British Embassy in the variegated splendours of Peking. Then Sir Charles Eliot, Ambassador in Tokyo, who had first engaged him from Ekaterinburg in 1919, helped to secure his future. For the moment he did not want to return to Britain; but what could he do? Sir Charles Eliot resolved his uncertainty by proposing employment in the Chinese Maritime Customs (its head was English), one of the principal sources of revenue on which the Government of China depended. Normally a Customs post involved a close study of Chinese which Gibbes did not want to pursue. Still, Sir Charles saw that, because of his Russian experience, he was specially considered; in the end he was appointed to Manchuria as an 'unclassed assistant', to help

Leave certificate in English, Russian and Chinese, attesting that Gibbes is an inspector in the Chinese Maritime Customs.

with awkward exchanges between the two Russian factions, Red and White, and the Chinese.

So Gibbes established himself in Harbin; engaged at first with a report on the last ten years' trading in Manchuria, and upon the general situation. Later he went to some of the outposts, in particular to remote Manchouli on the borders of Russia, Mongolia, and China: the place where one changed from the trans-Siberian line to the Chinese eastern railways. Tactically it was a key station. There was constant friction between the Soviet Consulate and White Russians employed by the Customs and much smuggling and infringement of currency regulations. Here Gibbes was an impartial mediator. Though he had been a member of the Imperial household, he contrived to get along well with the ex-convict Soviet Consul at Manchouli, a man who walked as if he wore chains on his legs, and who reacted fiercely when Customs men searched his baggage.

Twice Gibbes went up to Manchouli and managed to do much there for White Russian refugees. He had a term also – when for his health he lived on a six months' intensive starvation diet – at Lahosuso on the Sungari, a summer port only; no navigation when the river froze in winter. The Chinese at that hour found it very difficult to deal with Russians, and Gibbes had to be particularly diplomatic. He was happy. Harbin, full of Russians and with several English people in residence, gave him what social life he needed.

It was in Harbin that he met during 1922 a fifteen-year-old Russian boy who one day would be his adopted son and take his name. George Paveliev, Moscow-born, whose father was a civil engineer with contracts in the Far East, had gone in 1914 with his family to Nikolsk-Ussuryisk near Vladivostok. There he was at school for nine months. His parents, having business in Shanghai, took George with them and sent him to the Catholic boarding-school, St Francis Xavier. After the revolution he and his parents lost touch – though he heard from them in 1925 for the last time – and he completed his education only by the oddest freak. At week-end holidays he used to go aboard vessels in the port and talk to their officers and crews. Now he discovered a Russian boat, with a cargo of herrings, that was obliged to remain in harbour because essential dues were unpaid. Two of the pursers asked this eager, bilingual boy, then thirteen, whether he could help them to sell the herrings at the Chinese fish market. He did so, received two thousand dollars in commission, and was able to pay his own school fees and to stay at St Xavier's until 1922 when he travelled to Harbin. While working in one of the so-called junk-shops where the refugees brought their valuables, he met Gibbes, who helped to find him a job with an American fur company.

Gibbes looked ill in those days. But he was slim and impeccable in white or khaki suits, English-tailored, that never seemed to have been worn before; Harbin knew and respected him as the former tutor to the Tsarevich. Though as an official outside interests were barred, he was prepared to help White Russians, a courtesy that might have got him into trouble. He had lent money to the current leaseholder of the Harbin theatre, a relative of the Imperial Family's former chef. After a lapse of time and a complicated muddle of promissory notes, no one knew who really owned the theatre; it was unlikely that Gibbes would be repaid. George Paveliev heard from a barrister that the only thing to do would be to seize the building. By now George had raised in Harbin a troop of Sea Scouts after writing to Gibbes's older brother, William Arthur, a former Indian bank manager retired to Cornwall, for advice about methods and equipment; a troop of twelve, with the aid of a Chinese carpenter, built a schooner from a Chinese junk. It was in this spirit of adventure that George, with two Afghan friends, got Gibbes out of his difficulty by storming the theatre, capturing both building and cash-box, and triumphantly hoisting the English flag. In consequence, besides his job with the fur company, George acted for some time as theatre manager. Gibbes eventually got his money back.

When the hour came for English leave, he suggested that George might come too. Why not study for entrance to Cambridge? Not markedly studious, George preferred to be a farmer, and it was arranged for him to go to Australia where Gibbes had relatives. In the Philippines, on the way home, Gibbes was seriously ill at Manila; George hurried there immediately to nurse him for three months at Baguio in the mountains of Luzon, before seeing him off to England and travelling by himself to Melbourne. During that leave, and still conscious of his father's wish, Gibbes went back thirty years. He thought even now that he might enter the Anglican Church, but after concentrating on an ordination course at St Stephen's House, Oxford, during the Winter term of 1928 and the Hilary

George Paveliev, later George Gibbes, as a Sea Scout in 1924.

term of 1929, he had no strong call to proceed. With this chapter ended, he planned to return to China by way of Australia for the benefit of the long voyage. Before then he wrote from his sister's home, at Lea Marston near Birmingham, to the Serbian Minister in London.

In China, during the previous winter, he had visited Peking to see the tombs of members of the Imperial Family whose bodies had been removed from Siberia. These Romanovs had been interned in the small mining town of Alapayevsk in the northern Urals. On the night after the Ekaterinburg murders in July 1918, the Bolsheviks drove their captives out to a wood eight miles from Alapayevsk, bludgeoned or shot them to death, and threw the bodies down a disused mine-shaft. White troops found the bodies which General Dieterichs sent later to Peking when the district was evacuated. In Peking, so Gibbes wrote to the Serbian Minister,

> The coffins have all been placed in the crypt of the cemetery church which stands some little way outside the walls of the Northern (Manchu) City about fifteen minutes' rickshaw ride from the Russian Mission itself . . . I understand that the bodies were enclosed in nine caskets before being placed in their coffins. The coffins themselves are of the kind usually employed in Russian burials and are easily identified by means of small brass plates carefully affixed to each one. The names of the members of the Imperial Family who are still lying there, are: H.I.H. The Grand Duke Serge Mikhailovich, H.H. The Prince Johan Constantinovich, H.H. The Prince Igor Constantinovich, H.H. The Prince Paley.* Besides these were other coffins of persons who were attached to them. Unfortunately I have mislaid the notes taken at the time and am compelled to trust to my memory which does not extend to more than the principals.

Gibbes explained that the aged Archbishop Innokenty, head of the Russian Mission in Peking, though most sympathetic, lacked funds to do all that was needed; the church's fabric and roof must be repaired and a permanent priest appointed to say the offices for the dead. Hence Gibbes's approach to the Serbian Minister in London, who promised to do what he could, though 'the persons chiefly concerned' were now 'in very straitened circumstances'. At length the bodies were removed from Peking to Jerusalem and there reverently buried.

* Also murdered that night were the Empress's sister, the fervently devout Grand Duchess Elizabeth, and Prince Constantine Costantinovich.

The Sea Scouts' schooner.

Father Nicholas

In Australia, meanwhile, George, after a lively career on farms and sheep stations, was working as an insurance agent in Queensland. In 1931 he decided to go to England. Gibbes was also in England on leave, and he saw George set up on a Kentish fruit farm at Stourmouth, between Deal and Canterbury, which he would come to know very well himself. Soon he would be retiring from the Customs, but when in less than twelve months the Japanese invasion of Manchuria stopped him from finishing his term, he began seriously to consider the Russian Orthodox priesthood, a faith to which he was more and more attracted; indeed at Manchouli he had translated the service books into English. With some caution he spent a year in Shinto monasteries in Japan. The experience did not shake his resolve. On 25 April 1934, at the age of fifty-eight, he adopted the Orthodox faith, passing through his early degrees under the name of Alexis in the Tsarevich's honour; later, Archbishop Nestor of Kamchatka and Petropavlovsk, afterwards Metropolitan of Harbin and Manchuria, preferred him as a monk and ordained him to the Orthodox priesthood. Again assuming a fresh name, in honour now of Tsar Nicholas II, he began as Father Nicholas Gibbes the long final period of his life. He told the story in a letter written in two instalments (23 and 31 March 1935, New Style) to his sister Winifred. He explained first how during the previous December he had been made a monk, 'dressed in *my shroud*, a long white shift which covered me from my head to my feet'. It was a complex service in which, bowing to the ground and completely covered under two Archimandrites' mantles, he moved slowly along beneath their folds, his head bent to the level of his waist. The crowd in the church was so great that the procession had to fight its way through a dense mass:

I could feel it swaying from side to side, but actually I could

Gibbes soon after he entered the Russian Orthodox priesthood.

143

Archbishop Nestor and Father Nicholas.

only barely see the tiled pavement to which my head was bowed . . . Gradually we got to the Sanctuary steps, where again I bowed to the ground. Here I was given a taper by which I could just see well enough to read my portion of the rite. [*The Service continues*] . . . The obedience of the postulant is tested thrice. He is commanded to pick up the scissors which have been placed on the open copy of the Holy Gospels, and hand them to the Archbishop. This he does, at the same time kissing the Archbishop's hand. It is repeated twice; at the third time the Archbishop retains the scissors in his right hand while with his left he takes up a tuft of the postulant's hair. He shears it, and the action is done again in the opposite direction, the postulant being thus shorn cross-wise . . . [*Next, the vesting, and the creation of 'Father Nicholas'*] . . . I did not weep myself, but all the church was in tears. . . . I was overcome. [*He remained in the church all night, wearing mantle and cowl; at services during the following months he became deacon, priest, finally Abbot. At the last ceremony . . .*] When the discourses were over, the Archbishop blessed the people and vacated his place to me and I had to bless the people in my turn. The Archbishop returned to the Sanctuary and left me to complete this by myself . . . It took me more than half an hour, for there were several hundred people present. Like most ceremonies it ended in a cup of tea at the Archbishop's afterwards. Yours affectionately, + Abbot Nicholas.

The rest of a long life is soon told. Father Nicholas left Manchuria for the last time to spend a year in Jerusalem with the Russian Mission. Upon his return to England the Metropolitan Seraphim, Exarch for Western Europe, who was resident in Paris, attached him to a pair of London churches. They were All Saints in St Dunstan's Road, Barons Court (existing still) and, in Pimlico, a church lent by the Anglicans as the centre of the Russian Orthodox parish of St Philip: it gained some extra-mural celebrity from the singing of twelve Yugoslav girls who were known as 'the Belgrade nightingales'.

Father Nicholas developed into a leading Orthodox figure. In 1938 Archbishop Nestor, on behalf of the Exile Synod in Yugoslavia, created him an Archimandrite or Mitred Abbot, the first Englishman to be granted the additional honour of mitre and staff. This was at St Philip's; but presently the building in Buckingham Palace Road had to be sold, and later in 1938 Father Nicholas inaugurated in Bayswater Road a church for the English-speaking Orthodox community.

There he remained until the blitz on London. At this time many Russians, with several other Orthodox refugees from Europe, were living in Oxford: Father Nicholas, fitted by temperament to the life of a university town, promptly answered a call to create a congregation in the former medieval leper hospital of St Bartlemas on Cowley Road, beside Oriel College playing-fields. It became a thriving church that drew upon both university and town, and upon foreign language staffs of the B.B.C. from as far off as Reading and Evesham.

Five years later the war was over and Oriel again needed the chapel. Father Nicholas discovered a new home in Marston Street, also off Cowley Road in East Oxford. There he bought, with three cottages, a building that was once the home of an ancient charity founded to dispense free medicines to poor patients. To this day, given the correct slant of light, you can make out the word 'Doctor' under the paint of the library door. Until 1945 it had been the central A.R.P. telephone station for the whole of Oxfordshire; hence the sturdiness of pillars in the present church. For some years Father Nicholas maintained his work and preserved his relics of the Imperial Family: fine icons, one of which the Empress had given to him at Tobolsk and signed, and such personal relics as a pair of the ex-Tsar's long felt boots and a handkerchief, bell, and pencil-case owned by the Tsarevich.

By now Father Nicholas was a familiar figure in Oxford as he walked the streets with his tall staff and gold pectoral cross. The slim, immaculate tutor had changed to a venerable priest in Archimandrite's black robes with a spreading bush of white beard. His skin was remarkably clear and fresh; his eyes had a quick sparkle. Extremely sociable though he was, he could not often be persuaded to talk of the Imperial Family unless, perhaps, he was calling at Wadham upon Sir Maurice Bowra, whose father had been in the Inspector-General's department of the Customs; or at Headington, upon the Russian scholar, Dr George Katkov. He would stay with his hosts until the small hours, drinking strong tea without milk or sugar. Refusing to walk home in the darkness, he would wait sometimes until two or three o'clock for the moon to rise before he strode off, staff in hand, through a black and silver city. In advancing age (he was sixty-four when he reached Oxford) it was by no means simple to keep the church going. His authority and wisdom were honoured—in his day he had declined two important bishoprics—but though he

Father Nicholas.

ministered faithfully in Marston Street, he was obliged at length to entrust the services to visiting Serbian priests and to live for most of the time at his London flat by Regent's Park. It was a tiny place, much of it occupied by an elaborate sauna bath where, on occasion, he was known to spend an entire night. George, who lived near him, had left the Stourmouth farm at the beginning of the war because it was in a coastal district and he was still registered as an alien; since then he had served in the R.A.F. and had worked for several publishing houses.

During those last years Father Nicholas performed a final service to the memory of the Imperial Family. Yet again an 'Anastasia' appeared in Europe, and he agreed for once to see the claimant. His affidavit ran:

In the year 1908 I was appointed English Teacher and ultimately Tutor to the children of His Imperial Majesty Nicholas II of Russia and remained in Russia and with the Imperial Family for a period of ten years. As a consequence of my appointment, I was very familiar with the children of His Imperial Majesty, seeing them daily.

In particular, with my daily contacts with the Grand Duchess Anastasia, I was very familiar with her features and her hair.

On the 30 November 1954 I travelled to Paris with my friend Mr Michael Scott, who had made all arrangements for my travel, and for me to stay with a Mr Komstadius. We were met at the station with his car and taken to his house in the suburbs of Paris.

About the same time the person now calling herself The Grand Duchess Anastasia arrived from the Black Forest with her German companion and stayed in the house of Mr Komstadius.

After dinner I was taken for my first interview to the room the so-called Grand Duchess Anastasia and her German companion were occupying. The room contained two single beds in which the two women lay. They spent the whole of the five days in the house, and every time I saw them they were still in bed and I never saw them dressed at any time.

The so-called Grand Duchess Anastasia looked at me suspiciously over the top of a newspaper which she continued to hold on all occasions in front of her face so that only her eyes and hair were visible. This tactic she continued to use every time I saw her and never permitted me of her own will to see the whole of her face.

From behind the newspaper she stretched forth her hand and gave me the tips of her fingers to shake.

Such features as were visible did not correspond in any way with those of the Grand Duchess I had known, and I consider that, even bearing in mind the years that had passed between 1918 and 1954, the Grand Duchess Anastasia whom I knew could not have become anything like the woman now calling herself the Grand Duchess Anastasia.

It is true that her hair had been dyed, but nevertheless the texture of her hair was extremely coarse and fuzzy, whereas the hair of the real Grand Duchess Anastasia had been very fine and soft.

The so-called Grand Duchess Anastasia expressed no pleasure at meeting me again, made no recognition of me, made no conversation, asked me no questions, but merely answered questions I put to her. It was clear that she knew no Russian nor English which were the two languages always used by the Imperial Family, but on the contrary she spoke German only which was a language the true Grand Duchess Anastasia could not speak.

I shewed her six photographs which I had taken with me. She looked at each and shook her head and indicated that they meant nothing to her. These pictures actually were of some of the rooms in which the Grand Duchess Anastasia had lived, of the pet dog with which she had played, and of the teachers who had taught her.

I did not show her any pictures or photographs of the Imperial Family as she would probably have recognised them. I understand she had a collection of 2,000 postcards and photographs.

On the last time I saw the so-called Grand Duchess to say good-bye to her, I was able to approach nearer to her and look over the top of the paper, and saw her whole face and in particular her right ear. Her right ear does not in any way resemble the right ear of the true Grand Duchess Anastasia as I have a photograph of her which clearly displays the ear and its peculiar shape.

She in no way resembles the true Grand Duchess Anastasia that I had known, and I am quite satisfied that she is an impostor.

Two things he omitted. On arrival at the house he found that the claimant, on plea of illness, had asked everyone to wear masks, but there was none to hand. The second thing was a clinching proof of imposture. Thinking of Anastasia the sweep as she had appeared to him one morning long ago, Father Nicholas put a single question. Did the claimant remember what she wore when she came into his classroom at Tsarskoe Selo after a fancy-dress ball on the previous night?

'Yes,' she said without hesitation. 'I was a columbine . . . Wasn't I naughty!'

That, for Father Nicholas, was the end of another Anastasia.

The real Anastasia.

Epilogue

On 24 March 1963, two months after his eighty-seventh birthday, but indomitable to the last, Charles Sydney Gibbes, 'a clerk in Holy Orders (retired)', died in London at St Pancras Hospital. It was nearly fifty-five years since those few chance words by King Edward VII to the Empress in the sunshine of Reval had set him off upon his career as tutor to the Tsarevich. He is buried now in Headington Cemetery, Oxford.

Today the Warden of what has become St Nicholas House in Marston Street is his adopted son, George Gibbes. Since 1967 George has sought to preserve the building, and to continue the Orthodox services, in Father Nicholas's memory. In the church itself, where the ranked and beautiful icons speak for the faith of Holy Russia, there hangs an elaborate chandelier composed of three red and white glass tulips, a bunch of bronze flowers beneath them among a flourish of green and gold leaves. Half a century ago, it hung in the house of Ipatiev, the House of Special Purpose, in the bedroom shared by the four Grand Duchesses. Now it links an Oxford byway with the last days of the Imperial Family of Russia, and with that grim building fenced and guarded in the summer heat of Ekaterinburg.